Praise for *Higher Than Yonder Mountain*

Deany Brady's *Higher than Yonder Mountain* soars with brutal honesty and a deep love few ever experience, as well as heartbreak so deep you ache with her.

Wanda Dagraedt
Ellijay, Georgia

My book club has been waiting and hoping that Deany Brady would share with us the "rest of the story," and now here it is!

Ellie Roe
The Happy Bookers of Floyd, Virginia

I felt as though I was climbing with Deany Brady, and inwardly cheered each time she came out on top!!!

Wendy Minnes
Toronto, Canada

The little Deany that we all fell in love with in *An Appalachian Childhood* is back! From the glistening sands of Miami Beach to the bright lights of New York City, Deany comes full circle to the Appalachian home that gave her strength.

Susan Tidwell
Ellijay, Georgia

Brady's earnest, sweet charm guides her as she follows her "true north" wherever it takes her. In this beautifully written memoir, she digs down deep and not only reveals – but takes responsibility for – her darkest rock-bottom moments with unusual honesty and bravery.

Holly Thompson
Menlo Park, California

Deany Brady bares her heart and soul in this captivating account of her personal struggles, fairytale love story, fascinating friendships, and overwhelming grief, which transport the reader on the roller coaster ride that has been her life.

Lynelle Stewart
Ellijay, Georgia

I cried real tears during the most devastating parts of Deany Brady's story, written with such raw emotion that I could feel the deep, gut-wrenching grief come off the pages of her book.

Alicia Graham
Villa Rica, Georgia

I was reluctant to come to the end of Brady's rare collection of memories.

Rachel Gagnon
Watch Hill, Rhode Island

To: George,
I hope you
enjoy my book.
Best Wishes,

HIGHER THAN YONDER MOUNTAIN

Deany

by

DEANY BRADY

Dedication

I dedicate this book to the memory of three special loves of my life: my husband Jerry, and my dear friends, Ed and Sylvia Sullivan, godparents to our daughter Jeriann. These dear ones entered my life for a time and navigated me on a celestial cruise, but like all grand cruises, it ended too soon.

And the end of all our exploring will be to arrive where we started and know the place for the first time.

--- T.S. Eliot, "Little Gidding"

God enters by a private door into every individual.

--- Ralph Waldo Emerson

Character is what you are; reputation is what people think you are.

--- Mr. Hagan (My childhood mentor)

Contents

FOREWORD

In the first volume of my memoir *An Appalachian Childhood*, I told the story of my life, from my birth in a two-room shack in Appalachia to my young marriage with a traveling salesman in Atlanta, Georgia. The key figures in this story included my hard-working Mommy and Daddy, my loving Grandma and our encouraging neighbor Mr. Hagan. All of these people inspired my dream of a better life for both my family and myself. It was this dream that pushed me to leave my well known home and go out into the bigger world.

I grabbed the first chance I got to leave the farm by marrying Johnny and moving with him to the big city of Atlanta. He turned out not to be my savior, however, just an alcoholic, chain-smoking, unhappy man who could not hold a job. After many months of our suffering through a terrible marriage, I made a series of errors in judgement that almost ended my life. I had a brief affair that ended in a secret, dangerous back alley abortion.

Johnny decided to move to Michigan, believing that I would follow him. Instead, I knew I needed a new chance to make something good of my life, especially in order to help my family. I collected my meager savings and boarded a bus to Miami.

An Appalachian Childhood ends with me as a young woman in October 1953. Arriving at the bus station in Miami almost penniless, knowing no one, hungry and physically ill from the effects of the abortion, I set my foot on Florida soil for the first time to start the next chapter of my life.

PART I

My First Years in Miami

1: Arriving in Miami

I came to Miami with $16.22 in my pocketbook, and one suitcase, after the seven hundred mile journey on a Greyhound bus. I had bought my one-way ticket in Atlanta, hoping to put distance between myself and my unhappy married life. I felt sure that my only hope was to escape to a new city and start anew.

Still physically weak and emotionally distressed from the abortion, I had made this journey on my own, without letting anyone know, including my co-workers at the insurance company, my husband Johnny, or even my Mommy and Daddy. I had mailed my parents a letter that day from Pompano Beach, telling them I had left Johnny and intended to find a new job in Miami.

Although I had no idea where I would live in this city so new to me, I instantly felt buoyed up by the cheerful atmosphere and graceful architecture of the Miami bus station. This station looked much newer, bigger and calmer than the crowded one in Atlanta. Walking through the doors at midnight, I entered a spacious lobby with terrazzo floors and a high white ceiling. The many huge light bulbs, brightening the whole large room, caused me to have a fleeting thought that if Daddy were here he would be turning off a lot of lights.

Remembering how little money I had, I reassured myself that I would find a position soon, maybe at the Miami office of my old insurance company. I would have a good salary, and send home checks to my family. Maybe I would be able to begin evening college courses soon, and fulfill my dream of becoming a writer. I had come so far, from that little two-room house in the Appalachian mountains of Georgia, to the apartments I had shared with Johnny in Atlanta, and I hoped with all my heart to make a go of it here in Florida.

Clutching my purse in one hand and carrying my suitcase in the other, I returned from the bathroom and chose a seat two benches behind an older man, who was eating a sandwich. In this spot, I hoped I would not feel out of place eating the peanut butter sandwich I'd packed in my suitcase earlier that morning.

"Gee, that seems like a long time ago," I heard myself say aloud. I felt a little shocked at hearing my voice, and embarrassed too, since the man glanced my way. His warm smile assured me, though, that he was not annoyed and had not concluded I was a nut cake.

"Yes, one does lose track of time when traveling," he said, as he stood up, crumpled a wax paper wrapping and tossed it into a trash basket on his way out the door.

I felt grateful that he had spoken to me, especially since he sounded as if he thought I might be a frequent traveler rather than a person who had never before taken such a long trip. The farthest I had ever traveled had been the hundred miles or so between Atlanta and my family's home in Ellijay.

After finishing my sandwich, I drank some water from the fountain and lifted Johnny's old suitcase again. A cleaning crew with mops and a large pail of water was busy washing the floor nearby, so I went to a bench a ways behind them, where it looked like it had been freshly mopped, so that I could keep out of their way while they worked. Only a few passengers sat scattered about on benches near their luggage, some of them sleeping. No one paid any attention to me and no loudspeaker had spoken for some time. I was glad it was so warm that I didn't need a cover as I stretched my body out on the bench. My legs were swollen and sore from the bus ride.

I was so exhausted that I thought sleep would come easily, but I kept turning from side to side on that hard bench, thinking about my parents and Grandma at home. I worried about what they would think when they discovered what I had done. I knew I couldn't have stayed in my marriage, but I regretted so much: the hasty marriage itself, my arguments with Johnny over his drinking and his inability to hold a job, and my rebellious escape to the Biltmore Hotel that one dreamlike night, when I had gone to bed with the sweet-talking car salesman-preacher. I keenly regretted that I had gotten pregnant outside of my marriage, on that one occasion, and that I'd felt it necessary to have the illegal abortion, which had been so terrifying and had left me weak and distressed for months afterward, so that even now I did not have the physical energy and

17

health I should have felt, as a young woman of twenty-six. As I thought over all this on the bus station bench, I broke down and sobbed. Maybe coming to Miami had been yet one more disastrous decision. What if something awful happened to me here, and I didn't get back home to Georgia and to the security of my family?

Only a few people sat in this grand lobby, and my sobbing didn't seem to bother or even concern them. After all, who would care about a foolish woman who would take off to a strange city with no money? Maybe some people would have sympathy for me, as a pitiful runaway, but others might think of me as someone deluded, who should be put away and taken care of by people who were saner than I appeared to be.

I began to wish I had enough money to take the next bus back home and reach Atlanta before my parents received my letter. I thought that if I could only get back, I could make a collect call to Mr. Jones, the owner of the country store in Ellijay, a few miles from my parents' house. I knew since he was so fond of my Daddy and Mommy, he would offer to drive the whole way to the bus station in Atlanta and take me back home. This scenario was just a daydream, though. $16.22 would not be enough for a ticket home.

After a while, I must have drifted off to sleep, because a snarling male voice woke me up.

"This here'un looks ripe for the plucking."

I opened my eyes to see a heavily intoxicated young man hovering closely over me, smelling like alcohol. His short-sleeved

18

shirt displayed muscular arms covered with strange tattooed images of skulls, guns, and lewd words and images, such as I had never seen before, even in a picture. My first thought was that I was having a nightmare, but the young man's painful grasp on my shoulder was real. As I jumped to my feet, I saw a second man bending over me from the back of the bench.

This second one spoke in a whisper, saying, "Yes, I do believe you're right. This one looks ready." A thick reddish-brown beard covered the lower half of his face, and even though he spoke softly, his brown eyes looked wild. I raised myself to stand by the bench, but both men closed in, wedging me between them.

The one who had grasped my shoulder now put his arm around me as he said, "Oh, baby, don't be scared. You look like you could use a little fresh air. We got a real live automobile with wide open mufflers, waiting outside to wake you up."

The odor of their breath and bodies was so nauseating that I noticed it even in my state of terror. I couldn't see anyone to call for help, even if I could have found my voice. I caught a glimpse of a few people coming inside carrying their luggage, although they didn't seem to notice what was happening to me. Perhaps a bus was unloading, I thought, and more passengers would be arriving, although I hadn't heard the loudspeaker.

Right then, an alert young man in a soldier's uniform entered the lobby. As soon as he glanced in our direction, his steps quickened. Seeing the soldier moving toward us, the young man's tattooed arm fell to his side and both of my tormentors walked quickly toward the exit.

The soldier was now at my side. "Are you alright?" he asked.

"Oh, thank you!" I managed to squeak out. I thought my gasping breaths might turn into sobs.

He motioned me to sit, and then he sat near me, seeming careful to keep a few feet between us. I began to feel safe and my heartbeats became calmer.

"Before my wife arrives to pick me up, I'd like to introduce you to Security."

I had no idea what "Security" meant, but it sounded like safety. The soldier motioned for me to follow him as he approached a police officer, who was talking through a booth window to the ticket-seller. He introduced me to the ticket-seller, the officer, and a third man, whose tan uniform showed the word "Security" over a shirt pocket. After the soldier had told them about the behavior of the drunk young men, the police officer and Security shook my hand warmly, and the ticket man looked at me intently, as if to memorize my features in case he saw me needing more help.

A young woman now came rushing toward us, and the soldier waved to her, then turned to give me one more bit of advice.

"Should you be bothered again," he said, "just go over to the gentleman in the booth and he will contact Security."

"Oh, thank you, thank you," I said.

"Glen! Glen!" The young woman gave the soldier a big joyful hug, as happy tears ran down her cheeks.

I took my gaze away from them in this private moment. I was glad the soldier's name was Glen, because of my childhood friend Glen, who had also become a soldier. By the time my friend had gotten up the courage to give me my first kiss, I was a shy girl of sixteen and he was an "older man" of eighteen. I had often thought about him in the years since he had been killed in the War. Now, seeing this young soldier kissing his happy wife, it was as if my own Glen had forgiven me for my cautious and fearful response to his kiss, and had returned to bestow love on a young girl once again.

"I know you'll be safe," the soldier called back now, as he left the bus station, one arm around his wife and the other waving in a friendly way to me.

As I made my way among the empty benches, I kept glancing over at the man in the ticket booth, until I had come to a bench nearby, where a few people sat, including two employees of the railroad. The clock on the wall read 3:15 in the morning.

Once I was seated, my knees stopped trembling, but tears kept welling up as my throat seemed to close. I restlessly walked over to the water fountain to get a drink, although I found it difficult to swallow the water. I tried hard not to cry, because I didn't want anyone else but the ticket-seller to notice me. I yearned for my home and the sweet touch of someone in my family.

21

Too fearful to stretch out again and fall asleep, I tried to stay awake as I sat on the bench, holding the ticket-seller in my sight. I had been up for almost twenty-four hours and felt almost delirious from exhaustion. No matter how hard I tried to keep my eyes open, however, my eyelids closed again and again, and I dozed on and off during the next two hours.

Awakening, I looked at the clock. It was now 6:00 a.m., and I could smell coffee being brewed in the bus station cafeteria. My Mommy and Daddy would already be up having breakfast and planning their day of chores, and my co-workers in Atlanta would be getting up soon too. I reached into my bag and took out two nickels, mentally subtracting 10 cents from my small reserve, which left sixteen dollars, one dime and two pennies. I reminded myself to be sure and get two nickels for that dime from the woman in the cafeteria before I made the next phone call, so that I could have two nickels for future calls too. I had found that it was safer to have thick nickels instead of a thin dime, since you could lose dimes in the public telephone machine.

I needed to make a collect call to Mr. Jones and leave a message for my parents so they would know I was safe before the mailman came later that day with my letter. I knew Mr. Jones would be awake and busy, readying his merchandise before he opened the Cartecay Country Store. Of course, he never closed the store, since he was always available at his home just across the dirt road to anyone who knocked, day or night.

"He-low," he said.

The operator said, "Will you accept a collect call from Dean Brady, Sir?"

"Sure," he said, and as soon as the operator connected us he asked, "What's up, Odean?"

The first words I said were, "I will send you a dollar for this call in a letter to Mommy and Daddy as soon as I get a paycheck, Mr. Jones. Would you please go and tell my folks that I'm safe in Miami, and they'll get a letter today explaining why I'm here?"

"Well, uh...."

"Please, I don't have money to talk more. . . ."

A faint "Okay" came to my ear as I hung up.

With effort, I closed my mind as best I could so as not to worry about my family, and I went back to sit on the bench.

As an outgoing bus was announced, a man got up and left a *Miami Herald* on the bench. I rushed to grab it and flipped the pages to the want ads. Turning to the column "Rooms for Rent," I saw a vacancy: "Room with two meals." I took my dime to the cashier and she gave me two nickels.

I dialed the number, and after a couple of rings a woman's voice answered. When I asked her about the ad, she said, "Yes, the room is still available."

I released my breath, grateful that I had reached her, and that she was helpful instead of cross at this early hour in the morning. She carefully gave me the address, which I wrote down on a slip of paper. After I hung up, I went back to my seat and thought about how I would need more information on what buses to take to get there.

It was then that my calmness started to melt away again. How would I be able to figure out how to get anywhere in Miami? What if I got lost? A raging storm started up outside, with flashes of lightning, and I felt even more bewildered, as I sensed this big foreign city all around me.

Over the loudspeaker came the announcement of another bus arriving. It was now almost 7:00 a.m. Even though I could see no light outside, a sense of joy flashed inside my heart, now that I was experiencing my first dawn breaking over Miami. I didn't know what to expect here, but amid all the turmoil, I began to feel excited and hopeful.

A woman's voice said, "Let's sit here, where we can see him when he first comes through the door."

Looking up, I saw the woman with a teenage girl, both of them folding wet umbrellas and looking a bit uncomfortable with their dripping rain boots as they came nearer my bench.

Looking straight into my eyes, the woman's warm brown eyes were smiling, as she asked, "May we share your bench?"

"Sure, of course," I said, trying not to sound as overjoyed as I felt when a person spoke to me in such a kind voice on that lonely morning among strangers.

"My name is Doris and this is my daughter Judy." The woman nodded toward her daughter, who smiled at me.

"My name is Dean. I've just arrived from Atlanta." My voice wavered nervously as I spoke.

"Oh," she said, as if she were surprised that I felt the need to give her that information. "I'm from Georgia too. I married a Miamian and now we live on the other side of Miami, near the ocean – it's called Miami Beach."

"Oh, that's where I'm going to rent a room!"

I showed her the address I'd written down.

"I think I know about where that is," said Doris. "You'll enjoy that area a lot, I'm sure."

This start to our conversation seemed to establish a bond.

"Are you a student?" the woman asked me. "You look about the age of Judy, but I assume you're older, since you're here alone."

"I'm several years older," I answered, feeling pleased that I still looked so young, considering all the emotional and physical hurdles I had experienced over the course of the previous year.

"Judy and I are here to pick up my son, whose bus will arrive shortly. He's coming home for the holiday from a college in Tampa, where he's a student." Her voice sounded as sweet and promising as Christmas bells.

"Let's have breakfast," she said then, perhaps sensing that I was hungry. "I'd love for you to join us, Dean."

"Thank you so much."

I lugged Johnny's suitcase as I walked just behind Doris and Judy. Once we reached our table, Doris let her shoulder bump softly into mine as she helped me place my luggage beside my chair. It surprised me that she would even touch that old soiled suitcase.

My breakfast was a feast: two eggs over medium with a large slice of ham, plus grits with ham, and Southern-style "red-eye" gravy poured over the grits. (Red-eye gravy comes from frying ham meat and then pouring coffee into the hot pan after removing the meat.) It reminded me of Grandma's delicious breakfasts. The thought of my Grandma's cheerfulness each morning as she'd give us her biscuits and eggs, and sometimes a piece of sausage or bacon, almost brought tears to my eyes again.

When Doris paid for our meals, her generosity and caring overwhelmed me, and I was profuse in thanking her, to the point of making her feel slightly uncomfortable.

"Please," she said. "It's nothing. I'm happy you enjoyed it."

Soon after breakfast, her son arrived, and Doris and Judy rushed to hug him. I prepared to say goodbye to my new friends.

Instead, Doris introduced me to her son Daniel, and added, "We'll take you to your boarding house. It's on our way home."

"On a morning like this, sure, we must," Daniel said with a smile.

I was very happy about that and thought Doris and her family were surely my guardian angels. Doris wrote her phone number on a piece of paper, and I added this valuable paper to the other one in my purse, containing the boarding house address.

As Doris drove in the rain onto the Venetian Causeway – a long bridge crossing Biscayne Bay – all I could see was the gray, choppy water, which looked treacherous. The majestic hotels I had admired in pictures and magazines appeared to have been an illusion. Minute by minute, I became more grateful for that ride and more anxious about this new place.

Soon Doris pointed ahead. "This spot has an incredible view of the row of pretty hotels along the beach, but you can't see anything for the rain."

I felt relieved when she said that. Maybe I hadn't made a total mistake after all, and I would discover, as soon as the sun came out, that I had chosen my new city well.

The boarding house was difficult for Doris to find, since it was in a back alley behind an impressive building covered in terraces and overlooking the ocean. I imagined that such an awe-inspiring building must have nice and refined people living in it. In the future I would discover that this was even truer than I had imagined.

As I got out of Doris's car, I held tightly onto the two important pieces of paper, one with Doris's name and phone number, and the other, which I double-checked now, with the address of my new home. I walked up the front steps in the wet wind to ring the doorbell as Doris waited in the car, and soon a pleasant lady with short fluffy grey hair came out to greet me on the porch. She introduced herself as Stella, and said she was the person taking care of the boarding house.

"Call me tomorrow morning!" Doris called, as she backed up her car to turn around.

"Thank you, thank you," I cried, waving vigorously to her and her children with one hand, as I clutched the two precious pieces of paper in my other. In the flurry and excitement of the moment, however, I accidentally loosened my grip on the two papers, which flew wildly away. Watching the red tail of her car easing around the block, I realized that I couldn't contact this kind new friend in the morning, or ever.

Stella held my hand as she guided me inside the door. Once inside, she wrestled with the wind in order to close the door against the storm. Stella instantly reminded me of my Grandma, because of her warmth and her gray hair, although she wore her hair short, with her bangs softly covering her forehead above her bright blue eyes. My Grandma had never been to a hairdresser. Mostly both my Mommy and Grandma wore their long hair pulled up into buns.

Entering the living room of the boarding house, I blinked my tired eyes in an effort to accustom them to the bright lights. Three people were sitting at small individual tables, with breakfasts in front of them. They were intently watching the television news of the storm. The newscaster's clothes were almost taking leave of his body, as he stood in the wet, blustery wind.

Stella introduced me to Diana, Tom and Jonathan. She said I would soon meet Mildred too, who was already at work, and Vincent, who shared a room with Jonathan.

"These lovely young friends of mine will soon become your friends, I'm sure," she said kindly, "since we are a family here."

After we extended "pleased to meet you" greetings, she proceeded to lead me along a hall and then about six steps down to a lower level. We passed two washing machines and a dryer, all in action. I liked seeing those machines, since I would be needing my clothes washed. As we turned right at the corner into a very narrow hall, I wondered how I would ever find my way out again.

Soon Stella opened a creaking door. As we entered, she reached to pull a string attached to an overhead bare light bulb, allowing light to flood the large closet she called a room. A hand sink was on one side of the space, a half bed in the center, and a little table with a lamp on the opposite side. The furniture filled the room, so that it was difficult to walk a few feet in any direction. Stella opened a small door beside the table, which led into a tiny closet containing a shower stall and commode. A hanging rack with wheels, as in a clothing store, stood in a corner.

"This is not my house," Stella said. "My daughter Charlotte, who's out of town right now, leases this furnished house from the owner, and rents the rooms to boarders."

She then pointed to a half-window.

"That window will open about two inches, but since it's just above the garbage bins, the smell may be a problem." Looking at my disappointed face, she added, "I actually think of this little room as a transitional stop where young people stay briefly while they get settled and wait for a better room upstairs, as soon as there's a vacancy."

In her remark I sensed an apology and possibly a wish for me to have good luck so that I could afford a better place.

Rallying, I said, "This is just the kind of place I need for now, until I get paychecks after my transfer here. Besides, you look so much like my Grandma that I feel she may have been praying for me to have a warm welcome, and you are it."

She gave me a big hug and said, "God bless you, Dean."

"He already has."

She closed the door, waving a sweet goodbye. I collapsed into bed and fell into a deep sleep.

This was to be my home until I moved two years later and oh what a move that would be!

2: Paradise Found by Greyhound Bus

When I woke up, I turned to face the half-window. The garbage truck was making a racket outside, and I could see a crack of bright sun at the edge of the drawn shade. Rising from my narrow bed, I jerked at the string to turn on the light bulb. In the bright, bare light, I saw a small white clock, which Stella must have placed on the table while I was sleeping. The time was 3:00 in the afternoon of my second day in Miami. I had slept for more than twenty-four hours straight!

As I looked at the clock, I realized that something seemed unusual about it. When I lifted it to my ear I couldn't hear it ticking. Then I noticed an electric cord attached to it. My hand flew to my mouth, as I whispered, "I have an electric clock!" I had heard of such an astonishing device, but this was the first one I had seen.

Lying back on the bed, I started counting my blessings one by one, as my family's close friend Mr. Hagan had taught me. He said he had learned how important such a list of blessings was from the philosopher he and I both loved so much, Ralph Waldo Emerson. While my family frequently mentioned being thankful, it was not until I met Mr. Hagan, when I was a teenager, that I learned the value of actually naming my blessings each morning upon awakening – a habit I had let slip in the previous year, as my marriage with Johnny had crumbled.

My list of blessings started with my gratitude for my family and Mr. Hagan. I continued with thanks for a safe journey on the bus from Atlanta to Miami; for the kindness of the soldier; for Doris, who had brought me safely here; and for the graciousness and caring I had already received from Stella. Gazing at the ceiling, I expressed extra thanks for a safe, dry shelter, where I would also have two meals a day.

The ceiling held a huge spot, like a dark cloud. It reminded me of the places on the ceiling of my childhood home, where rain had leaked through the newspapers placed there for insulation. I remembered how, when I was a child, such leaks had caused me no worry, since I had been too small to read the ceiling anyway. One of my greatest pleasures had been to read the newspapers covering our walls, which we refreshed each year with bundles of old papers from our wealthy neighbor Mrs. Leach. For my Mommy and Daddy, this wallpaper helped keep us safe and dry, yet for me they created a window into the large, exciting world of celebrities and adventure.

Feeling strengthened by my grateful thoughts and vowing I would not ever forget to create a list of fresh thanks each morning in Miami, I scampered around to figure out what I could wear. I decided I would just try to look the best I could in my wrinkled skirt and blouse. Glancing out the door into the dimly lit hallway, I could see a folded ironing board near the washing machine, and an iron on top of the dryer -- more blessings to be counted! After I had ironed my clothes and gotten dressed, I started to walk through the maze of crooks and turns, soon reaching the upstairs.

Waves of salty ocean air from the open window touched my face and sent soothing balm through my entire body. The blue sky shone clear, with just a few white clouds floating high up. The modern look of the living room, lit up by the sun, contrasted with any home I had known, including Johnny's and my second apartment in Atlanta, which had been pretty but older. The large tan sofa and two matching stuffed chairs looked so new by comparison to my family's old furnishings, like my Grandpa Will's homemade cabinet. I wondered how many blessings I might be able to count by nightfall.

The living room was peaceful and empty now. I noticed a shiny black telephone, quite a contrast to the dirty, oil-smeared one in Mr. Jones' store. People using this boarding house phone clearly had clean hands, while our neighbors often used the store phone in Ellijay for emergencies, as when someone skidded off the muddy dirt road and landed their vehicles, usually pick-up trucks, in a ditch. I wished my parents had a phone too, so I could call them directly instead of having to go through Mr. Jones.

I hoped my Mommy and Daddy were alright and not worrying about me. By now they would have received my letter and my reassuring phone message. I promised myself that I would send them my new address as soon as I could. I would tell them that I now had a safe place to live, right near the water in Miami Beach.

I couldn't help wondering whether I had been right not to tell my family ahead of time that I was leaving. I knew for sure, however, that if I had told them, I would have caved in to their wishes and stayed close to home in Georgia. Standing in the living room of the boarding house, I decided that I had acted in the best way possible, because my family had not had to worry until I arrived here, and now I would be in a position to make all our lives more comfortable.

Looking through the huge plate glass windows, I saw Stella and three of the guests relaxing on lawn chairs in the small, neatly kept garden. Stepping outside, I walked along the pebbled path to greet them. As we exchanged smiles and friendly hellos, I pulled up a straight, white wooden lawn chair to join them. The white chair looked just like one I had seen in the summer home of Mrs. Leach, the Coca Cola heiress, in my childhood. I couldn't help but lose myself a moment, remembering how good I had felt, sitting in one of Mrs. Leach's chairs, after I had spent hours dragging the limbs Daddy and Mommy had trimmed from her trees. They would pile all the extra brush together in an open spot on her land, and then they would light it, like a bonfire. Often, once the fire had started, Daddy would toss in an old car tire that couldn't be repaired, which would fuel the fire to such an extent that it would almost burn my face, as I sat enjoying the flames.

Chatting with Stella and my fellow boarders, I realized how often, in these last few days, I had thought about Mrs. Leach and Mr. Hagan, the two people outside my close-knit family who had helped me envision a better life. I realized that because each of them had encouraged my dreams, I felt their presence intensely now, as I was watching those dreams start to become real. Even though I had no job yet in Miami, and my room was small, I had come hundreds of miles, all on my own, to this promising and luxurious new place, and had already started to feel at home here.

I was startled into attention when I noticed that the other guests and Stella had been looking at me expectantly. I sensed they might be a little curious about the newest member of their group.

Smiling, I let my glance gratefully take in their circle, as I said, in what I now realized was a Southern drawl, "Please excuse me, I'm still not quite awake. I was so tired after my long trip, I've been sleeping for hours."

Thinking I should say something nice to my hostess, I looked at Stella and said, "Now, thanks to you for my nice comfortable bed, I am well rested."

My remark started an hour or so of conversation, as I ate my lunch from a full tray Stella had saved for me. While we talked and laughed, I tried to memorize the names and features of Diana, Jonathan, and Tom. I told them about my hope that the Miami branch of the insurance company for which I'd worked in Atlanta might have a job for me.

Tom, a good-looking middle-aged man from Michigan, with unusually long brown hair streaked with silver, said, "That building is just a block from where I work. I'll be glad to take you there. I could also bring you back with me at five o'clock."

I was almost speechless with joy, but managed to say calmly, "Thank you so much!"

In the next instant, I tucked away a needling worry that Tom might be romantically interested in me. After all that had happened to me in my marriage, I felt vulnerable.

Stella said, "That's marvelous, Tom."

It flashed into my mind, how Mrs. Leach had used that word "marvelous" to describe me when I was a little girl. Now I was among people who used such words on a daily basis.

At five o'clock the following day, I left the office of the insurance company, relieved that I had indeed secured my job there with a new boss, Mr. Clarkson, who looked like a generous person. He and my immediate supervisor, Mrs. Hammel, had made me feel right at home. I felt good, having heard the nice things Mr. Hawkins, my boss in Atlanta, had said about me. He had given this office a glowing account of my work ethic and my enthusiasm.

Mr. Clarkson smiled. "He said that you would be a definite asset to our office staff."

I felt so touched that tears came into my eyes.

Mr. Clarkson had also smoothed the way for me, in terms of my debt to my former boss.

"Mr. Hawkins mentioned that you had an illness last summer," he said, "causing the need for you to borrow $400.00 from him. He suggested I should let enough time go by for you to have four paychecks before we start taking a small amount from them each week."

Mr. Hawkins' kind words made it sound almost an afterthought that I owed him $400.00. I was grateful he had not known the truth about my personal debt that I needed the money for my abortion, although I wondered if he had guessed.

For the second time that day, I went to a bench in a small park a block from the insurance company, beside Biscayne Boulevard. Tom had designated that spot for our meeting at lunch, and now at 5:30 I was on the same bench waiting for him to collect me for my ride back to the boarding house. As his light blue convertible approached, with the top rolled back, the sun shone on his smiling face and his graying hair. I suddenly felt more secure in his presence, confident that he simply liked me as a friend and would not press for intimacy.

He eased to a stop and I hopped inside. Feeling light and happy, I said, "What a thrill, to ride in a convertible."

"A beautiful girl like you will be experiencing a lot of smooth sailing rides in convertibles now, since you're in Miami."

He turned onto a bridge that looked a mile long across the bluest water. Until that moment, I had never been able to picture clearly the vastness of an ocean, yet now, from this bridge, I could see how infinite it looked.

Gazing at this blue expanse, I was reminded of a Sunday afternoon in our two-room house, when I was working my six-year-old brain trying to understand what the preacher had said that morning in church. Grandma and Mommy were sitting together on the porch, as Grandma churned clabbered milk, moving the dasher up and down in the churn, in the process of forcing the butter from the milk. Mommy had her aproned lap filled with the green beans she was stringing.

I was sitting on the floor at their feet, when I asked, "Grandma, what did the preacher mean when he said, 'After forgiveness, God will cast all your sins into the bottom of the sea?'"

Grandma said, "It's just a Bible saying that means something like if you pray for forgiveness of your sins, you will be freed from them, and God would push them under all that water and you'd never have to think of them again. . . . Mamie, I can't explain what the preacher said, you take over."

"No, Mommy, you're doing good explaining it." She smiled a little mischievously. "The only thing I could add would be that a big whale like the one that swallowed Jonah could swallow your sins and later bring them up to land and heave them onto the shore."

Mommy was being funny, and I loved her for it, yet I most appreciated how Grandma had tried so hard to clear up my muddled thought about that Bible passage. On the bridge with Tom now, I smiled to myself, thinking I hoped Grandma had been right, that all the things I regretted could be buried under the sea, invisible and forgotten. I wouldn't want them coming back up onto the shore.

"How did it go with your job?" Tom asked now.

"Oh, I can't believe I didn't blurt out my good news first thing! I got the transfer. It went very smoothly. Yes, I'll be employed tomorrow."

"Well then, we shall return together tomorrow."

Tom grinned, and I was sure once more that he thought of me as a young person under his wing, and not as a potential girlfriend.

"Oh, good, and I must pay for gas," I said, thinking of the $16.02 I still had in my purse.

"Nope, I'm coming this way anyway," he said. Not giving me time to respond, he went on, "I'm not being a proper tour guide. I need to be telling you we are traveling on the MacArthur Causeway."

"I just cannot tell you how much I appreciate your kindness."

Tom waved away my gratitude, and grinned again. "So tell me about what happened at your new office today."

"They were so nice, and my new boss Mr. Clarkson told me their file clerk left yesterday to be a cocktail waitress in one of the big hotels."

"You were lucky to arrive at the beginning of the tourist season," Tom said. "That's the way it is here in Miami. When the winter season opens, stenographers leave their steady jobs in Miami and go by droves to find work in the big hotels. They're looking to make a killing and live high on the hog until May, when the tourists leave."

I smiled, thinking how Southern "high on the hog" sounded. I had heard this expression many times, but I was surprised to hear Tom saying it in his Northern accent. I found his words a bit difficult to understand sometimes. It never occurred to me that he might have trouble understanding me!

"Now, as we leave the MacArthur Causeway, we turn onto Collins Avenue. Prepare yourself to experience a real live fairy tale as we drive through the majestic row of hotels. Biscayne Bay, the yacht harbor, is to our left. To our right is the glamour and glitter of Miami Beach on the coast of the great Atlantic."

Looking at that blue ocean, I thought how it looked as if it joined the sky "way out yonder." Strange birds, such as I had never seen before, circled and circled, dipping their long beaks into the water before landing on posts.

"Why those constant dips of their beaks into the water?" I asked Tom.

"They're grabbing food – small fish swimming just below the surface."

"Perhaps I might have figured that one out if I had spent a little time thinking about it," I said with an apologetic touch.

"I'm happy to answer any questions you have, Dean. Ask away."

I daydreamed for a moment about Grandma, and how many times she had said, "Children, this little branch you are wading in will be in the big ocean one day. I wonder what that ocean looks like."

"I must bring my family here," I said to Tom.

He nodded and smiled. Although he was too nice to say so, he was probably thinking that I would have to have a better paying job than that of a file clerk, if I hoped to spend money on my family. My mind, however, was exploding with thrilling thoughts so loud I could almost hear them in the silence -- thoughts, the likes of which had kept my "impossible dream" alive, of a more plentiful life for my family and me. The wild ideas circled around and around, just like the beautiful birds: *I am now in a city made of pure gold. I am not looking at dream images. This grandeur I could touch, and soon I will have lots of money to hold in my hands.*

I pictured the first thing I would buy: a new pair of glasses for Grandma. She could hardly see with the ones she now had. The tiny screws had fallen from the frame and she had to wind a string around the ear pieces to keep them on her face.

A few days later, returning from work with Tom, I saw an envelope addressed to me in Mommy's handwriting. I had always thought she had good handwriting, considering she had had so little "schooling." As I tore into the envelope, out fell two letters. One was from Mommy and the other – written on a crumpled, soiled piece of lined notepaper – was the only letter Daddy had ever written to me; in fact, although I could not know this on that day, it would be the only letter he wrote to me in his entire life. Both letters were filled with thoughts about how worried my parents were for me, and how much they missed me.

Though it was difficult to decipher Daddy's letter, I made out his opening words:

I'm sitting here on my praying stump at the top of the mountain field patch, praying to Jesus to send you safely back home.

Not wanting anyone to see me cry, I briefly greeted Diana and Jonathan, who were sitting in a friendly circle, making room for Tom and me. I told them I was going to take a walk along the public beach they had shown me, only a short block down Collins Avenue.

Stella called out from the kitchen, "Dinner will be served at 7:00, about an hour from now."

"I'll be back before then," I said, feeling grateful to Stella for the healthy meals she gave to us.

Much as I appreciated my fellow boarders' friendliness and the blessing of food, the sense of family I had been developing over the past days with Jonathan, Tom, Diana and Stella was fast weakening, with news of my real family right before my eyes. As I walked, feeling the soft salty moist breezes, I kept kissing my parents' letters. Looking back, I saw Diana walking toward me.

Coming closer, she said, "Stella was afraid you might get lost, and since I felt like a walk, I followed you."

"Thank you very much," I said. "I'd love your company, since I'm lonely for my family."

We sat on towels Diana had brought and had a companionable talk. She told me that she was a cocktail waitress in a popular hotel a few blocks away. My ears perked up as she mentioned her large salary. Hearing about all the big money that people were making in the hotels, I started thinking of a plan. I asked Diana about the possibility of working evenings there.

"Have you ever served as a cocktail waitress?" she asked.

"No, and I've only been inside one bar -- the Biltmore Hotel in Atlanta." I hoped Diana wouldn't ask me anything about that visit, which had led to such sadness.

"Well, maybe you might should do as I did when I moved here last year. Since I wasn't experienced in this type work, I realized I wouldn't be likely to be hired in a big sophisticated cocktail lounge."

I listened intently while she told me that to get experience she had worked for one year in a bar just across the Venetian Causeway, in Miami, and she had made good money there.

"In fact, I could introduce you to the boss," she said. "He's very nice and a good friend."

I agreed, so the next evening when I came home from work, we slid into her Chevy Corvette and off we went to the bar. The ride was pure heaven, as I felt my body melting into the comfortable seat covers.

Her friend Bill was happy to meet me and immediately asked if I would like to work evenings. He offered to teach me how to waitress, and told me I would make a lot of money in tips, in addition to my salary. He also said he would be glad to take me home, since my boarding house was on the way to his own house in Miami Beach.

He turned to Diana and teased her. "You remember us having nice rides home when I dropped you off at your boarding house last year, before you bought your fancy sports car?"

"Yes, and I can no longer doze off anymore, since I have to drive!"

He told me the number of the bus that would bring me straight down Biscayne Boulevard from the insurance company to the bar. Eager to make money and too naive to be afraid, I agreed to work in the evenings from seven until eleven. Two days later, I would begin my career as a bar girl.

To celebrate my good luck with securing my transfer to the insurance company and now landing an extra, higher paying job, the next evening after work I decided to go to the beach again. I felt drawn to that big, glittering ocean. On my way there, I stopped by a mailbox and dropped in a letter to my parents. Not wanting them to worry about me working in a bar, I copied what Diana had told her parents back in New Jersey: "I have had good luck and have landed a job as a model." I could imagine Mommy telling the neighbors that her daughter was now a model. This lie seemed innocent enough to me.

Since it was already dusk, the beach was deserted, but I could still see many tracks in the sand, indicating that people had been there when the sun was shining. In the quiet, I listened to the soft, slow splash of the ocean and felt that all the turmoil of my life in the past couple of years was washing out to sea with the waves. I dug my bare heels into the sand and, with a tinge of homesickness, said a fond goodbye to Georgia. I thought about the poem I loved, by Henry Rootes Jackson:

> *The red old hills of Georgia!*
> *So bald, and bare, and bleak --*
> *Their memory fills my spirit*
> *With thoughts I cannot speak.*

To my mind, the near impregnable red clay represented being poor, with not enough nutrients to support life. I felt that this Miami Beach seascape and shoreline, with its graceful hotels and people in convertibles, was so much richer in all ways. I relished the warm sand under my bare feet as I watched the boundless waves. To me, the vastness of the ocean and the billions of grains of sand represented infinite abundance and prosperity.

My Daddy, Mommy and Grandma struggled with that red clay all their lives. Without a doubt I would never meet anyone who worked harder than they did and with such honesty and integrity. Of course, they would not have described their daily chores with that big word "integrity." They would simply have defined their work as "honest labor." In honor of their striving to give me an education, I felt glad to be able to use that word to describe them. Thanks to my family, I knew the meaning of so many words, and I didn't have to go as often now to Mr. Hagan's dictionary to look them up.

The image of rolling that die in the office in Atlanta came back to me. Which city would it choose for me: New York, Washington, D.C., or Miami? Remembering the die spinning on the desk and coming up with just one dot, for Miami, I sent my words out on the ocean breeze: "Thank you, die, you chose well for me."

3: Bar Fly Girl

At first I was so happy to be making extra money as a bar girl that I could almost ignore the cheap look of the place, the smells and the job-induced nausea. Bill, the owner of the bar, was a friendly and handsome man of about forty who said his ambition as a child had been to become a movie star. Evidently he had had some success, since various photographs on the walls showed him acting in a small part in *Key Largo*, a movie that had been filmed in the Florida Keys.

The bar's outside white walls were badly in need of a new coat of paint. The stucco in many places had worn thin or broken off, and the white color had become dirty. Inside, the bright green walls were dark from years of cigarette smoke. Chairs and tables looked mismatched, as if they had been bought from a second hand store. Bill kept the bar itself clean and polished, though, and the bottles glinted in front of the mirror.

Libby, the other bar girl, helped teach me the ropes. She was tall and slender, with long reddish brown hair. She looked twenty years older than I was, but I knew she was probably only in her mid-thirties. When she opened up a few times to talk about her childhood, it became clear that she had had a rough road as a child. Her mother had abandoned her and she grew up living with her dad's half-brother, since her own dad was in prison serving a life sentence for robbery and murder. One relative had sexually abused her. She would break into tears at this point in her story, and I never pressed her for more details.

Libby walked as if she were imitating the sexy moves of Marilyn Monroe's famous stride. The comparison to that curvy actress, though, ended with the walk. For one thing, Libby was as skinny as a piece of ragweed. I hardly ever saw her eat any food, but I gathered that earlier in the day she always had a Coke in front of her – that is, until she moved to strong drinks just before lunch. She told me she had been addicted to Coke ever since she had lived with her uncle, a migrant farmer whose children and Libby would search the area, each time they moved, to find the nearest store selling Coca Cola. Her soulful blue eyes were so hauntingly beautiful that one could easily get lost in them and ignore the dark blue circles underneath. Learning of Libby's experiences made me feel even more grateful for the love my family had showered on my sister, brother and me.

My first lesson as a "bar fly," right from the start, was a simple one: how to breathe while detaching myself mentally from the smoky alcohol breath of customers. After my marriage to Johnny, who had filled our apartment in Atlanta with the smell of cigarette smoke and beer, I felt sick at the least hint of those odors, yet I managed to become proud of my ability to hold a fake smile for hours while gazing into the face of some miserably lonely stranger.

My job was to sit on a stool in high heels and a form-fitting dress, in order to entice the male customers to buy drinks for me (actually pretend ones) as they ordered more and more drinks for themselves. Seeing a customer seating himself on the opposite side of the circular bar, I would lift myself off my own stool and move closer to him, just as Libby had shown me how to do.

"May I sit with you?" would be my opening remark.

Usually the stranger would be lighting a fresh cigarette off the one he was about to snuff out, and even in the dim lighting, I would be able to see how his fingers were dark yellow from nicotine, like Johnny's. The customer would signal to Jesse the bartender to bring him a drink, often a straight bourbon, and then he would order whatever drink I said I would like. I mostly asked for a bourbon, and Jesse, following his usual method, would dip a glass quickly into a shallow bowl of bourbon, pour it out, and then fill the glass with ginger ale. In this way, should the customer become suspicious that I might not be drinking the alcohol he had paid for, he could smell it on my glass.

Bill helped keep the situation safe. Whenever anyone put their hands on us girls in a lustful way, Bill's habit was to place himself immediately behind the bar to serve drinks, keeping his eye on the customer, and soon the man would stop. Otherwise, Bill would quietly ask him to leave. This approach was to Bill's advantage, because he could sell more drinks if his bar girls sat upright, instead of succumbing to someone's advances and asking to

49

leave early on a date. Whatever Bill's motivation, I was glad that he kept such a close watch on the customers, in case they tried to touch me.

As I appeared to listen eagerly to one customer after another, I often had occasion to be grateful for my childhood experiences on the farm. My chores had helped me gain a strong stomach and a valuable work ethic. One of my biggest jobs as a little girl had been to retrieve the dead animals from under the floor of our house -- a job for which I was chosen because I was the smallest. Daddy and Mommy trained me well in how I should make my way, following the scent of the decaying animal. Once I had discovered the cold, stiff creature, I would grasp one of its legs and begin the process of pulling it toward the daylight. Experiences like this one had surely been useful in preparing me to tolerate hard or upsetting tasks in my life, including talking with the drunks in this Miami bar.

I often had to remind myself of Diana's encouragement, as she had told me how helpful this job had been for her, in preparation for her job at a cocktail lounge. As she had promised, I earned good pay. I also reminded myself of Mr. Hagan's words: "Let every experience in life be a learning experience." It seemed an eternity since Mr. Hagan had introduced me to his library and to the inspiring essays of Emerson, yet as I met my first customers in Bill's Bar, I felt consoled by the thought that even in this situation I could still gain insight into the life around me.

I quickly learned that most of the customers' conversations followed the same pattern. After a brief greeting, one of them would start in with the usual "What's a beautiful young girl like you doing in a place like this?"

Without pausing to listen for an answer, the customer would then launch into a sea of complaints, sprinkled with compliments for this bar girl at his elbow.

"You take my wife, she yells and screams at me and the kids all the time, and I tell you I can't remember her ever sitting and listening to me as you do. You are a beautiful little angel."

Taking a sip of my ginger ale, I would move the muscles of my face in an effort to brighten my fake smile. I tried to erase any thoughts of my parents and my Grandma, who would have been so distraught to see me in such a place, spending my energy on people who should have been at home with their families.

Each night after the bar closed and Bill drove me home, I would look eagerly for a letter from Mommy, on the table where Stella carefully sorted the mail each day. Mommy wrote regularly once a week with bits of news about each member of the family, including the two cows, the horses and the dogs. She most always added a message from my Grandma, telling me how Grandma wished I could have sat with them at dinner that day and eaten her good green beans and half-moon pies. Daddy's messages always seemed to go back in time, to when I'd worked in the fields with him. Often his message went something like this: "Tell my little

51

Cotton-top that Charley looked sad today, because he missed her riding on his back to and from the fields."

The horses, Charlie and Frank, had replaced the mules, John and Jean, who had aged and died some years earlier. Each time one of the animals died, we mourned for them somewhat as if they had been family members.

I was especially anxious for news of my Grandma, since Mommy had started to mention that Grandma had been experiencing difficulty breathing. In one letter, Mommy said Grandma had been "having spells of smothering." ("Smothering" was a Southern expression meaning "shortness of breath," or difficulty breathing.) Oh, how I longed to have my Grandma living with me in Miami, and breathing the pungent salty ocean air.

Sometimes, as I pretended to listen to my customers' stories and complaints, I couldn't help remembering the rare nights when my own Dad had come home late, staggering from sampling his moonshine after having distilled a small batch. Mommy's unshakable patience had a workout as she would try to calm him enough so that he could lie down and she could massage his forehead.

"It feels like a tightrope is being pulled around my head," Daddy would say.

Then in his misery he would raise his skinny, muscular body from the bed to pace the floor, threatening to get his mule and "ride this spell out."

Those nights had not happened often, but when they had, I had trembled in my bed as I snuggled next to Grandma, who also trembled fearfully. She and I would hold each other close, as we listened to Daddy cursing people and things in his life situation -- outbursts so different from his usual peaceful attitude of accepting his problems.

After those awful nights, Daddy would awaken the next morning, so sad for his binge of the night before. Upon seeing him, I would rush to hug him. That was not the way my sister Colleen reacted, however. She never forgave him. But Grandma would always remind us, in the wake of one of those traumatic nights, "Children, don't hold any bad thoughts about your Daddy. That was not him speaking; it was the devil speaking through him." I wondered if my customers' families could feel forgiveness for these husbands and fathers getting drunk at the bar, as Grandma felt for her son-in-law.

Since Bill drove me home each evening after the bar closed, I would wait while he and Jesse cleaned the bar.

Once I asked, "May I help with washing the glasses? I'm good at that."

"Oh, no, Dean," they chimed in together. "You've got to keep your hands soft to the touch."

The irony of Jesse and Bill taking care of my hands struck me, because I was smiling with the men each evening, while I was perhaps robbing their children of something better in their own lives.

One August evening, almost a year after I had come to Miami, wild winds shook the bar in a thunderstorm, while my companion for the hour was describing how his wife had run away with their two children. Sometimes sobbing through the details and just as quickly expressing angry threats toward his wife, he seemed oblivious to the storm. Two times he slid off his barstool, and then stood, holding onto the bar for support. The second time, he drunkenly apologized for his foul language.

"Bartender, I want to apologize to these nice people who I might be bothering and give a round of drinks to everyone. I'm a gentleman, really. I was taught by my parents to respect women, but they had not then met such a bitch as I married. Jesse, make a round of drinks for everyone, including me and my sweet girlfriend here."

He curved his arm around my shoulder and began to tighten his hug. However, Bill immediately shot him a sharp stare, and my drinking partner quickly loosened his arm and let it down to grasp his glass. He raised the glass to his mouth, gulping a couple of swallows. Then he sat beside me again, venting his personal thunder more quietly now, but still, to my ear, storming for another hour above the noise of the storm. I couldn't be sure how much time had passed, because Bill always moved the clock into the kitchen, so that customers would stay and drink more. My "date" had run up a bar bill of almost five hundred dollars, having ordered for himself and other customers countless bourbons, beers, and a variety of mixtures, including Scotch and Coke, and one Scotch and milk for someone who had stomach ulcers. All this time, I had slowly sipped two ginger ales, holding a pleasant thought in my mind as I figured out how much my percentage of his bill would be. My tip each night was forty per cent of what my customers spent, adding significantly to the modest salary I made at the insurance office each week.

That hefty tip of two hundred dollars temporarily lifted my spirits when the customer left, although my low-grade nausea had escalated so greatly that I had to go into the bathroom and throw up. Still on my knees, with my elbows pressing on the toilet seat and my fingers pinching my nose against the stench, I opened my eyes. As I noticed the dried crud around the inside of the bowl, more vomit slushed from my mouth. Finally getting up, I went to the bathroom, only to realize that the flushing mechanism had broken, so now my urine would remain in the toilet bowl, mixed with my vomit. Luckily the tiny rusty sink allowed a rush of water so I could at least wash my face and hands.

Staring at my tired face in the tiny mirror, I pulled the roll of cotton fabric down from the dispenser and found a small clean spot on which to dry my hands and face. I spoke to myself, my words echoing in the empty bathroom.

"Why am I doing this?" I said. "Am I really doing this for the lessons I can learn?" I raised my voice and almost yelled to my reflection. "Hell no! I am doing this for the cold, hard cash!"

By the following morning, though, once the sun had come out again and the seagulls floated over the ocean, I felt happy about the big tip. That $200 meant that I could send a large money order home, and still put a good amount into my savings account for college. I continued on as a bar girl, hoping that one day I would really start my education.

The question of whether this job was worth it needled me, though, and often I felt on the brink of giving it up. The work had a disturbing side to it that I found increasingly hard to ignore. Often my older co-workers, including Libby, took temporary sexual partners upstairs to a bedroom. When I would go into another little bedroom behind the bar, to rest for awhile, I could hear noises from the room upstairs. I could also hear Libby or the other girls making artificially sweet comments to someone about how great the sex had been, and that depressed me.

I had never even seen the upstairs, and this fact pleased Bill. I think it raised my value in his eyes. In fact, I had not seen any customer in the bar who looked at all appealing to me.

One day, however, a most handsome and energetic young man entered the bar and came straight over to sit by me. His charming smile gave me a wave of joy.

"Hi," he said cheerfully, as he reached for my hand. "I'm Jack. What's your name?"

"I'm Dean," I said, beaming with a glow giddier than I had ever experienced before.

Bill soon appeared, and said, "How good to see you, Jack. We've been missing you."

"I've been living in our villa in France for the past year. It's very good to be back, especially since I've found adorable Dean here." He bent toward me and said warmly, "Dean, let's you and I go sit at that corner booth and get acquainted."

Bill hastily carried our drinks to what quickly became "our booth."

After this first meeting, Jack invited me to have a regular booth date with him almost weekly, and our time together became the height of joy. I walked with a bounce that had not been typical of me for at least two years. To my eyes, Jack looked almost identical to Cary Grant. His mannerisms were just as polished, and his voice as melodious. His thoughtfulness and generosity, along with his sober behavior, caused much happiness to surface inside me, and I was beginning to feel that my life might be close to making a bright turn. I assumed that Jack was married, since he never mentioned a date outside our booth, yet I still felt increasingly hopeful that something good could happen.

One summer night, underneath a gorgeous Miami moon, as Bill drove me home through the warm city, he whistled the tune to "Stay as Sweet as You Are."

At a red traffic light, he turned to face me, and said, "You know, Dean, your youth allows you to be far more in demand than the older girls, and your bouncing ponytail excites the men."

I felt embarrassed to hear Bill talk about my looks in this way, and I couldn't think what to say.

Bill went on, "You take Libby. She was beautiful only a couple of years ago, but she started drinking and going to bed upstairs with my customers, and now she's not of much value to me. I wish she would quit, because she's not making any money for me while she's in bed. I know you like her a lot, Dean, but she's a mess."

I felt surprised and upset that Bill could talk about Libby this way. Usually he spoke more nicely. As we crossed the Venetian Causeway, heading home, though, I realized that in fact Bill and I hardly ever talked at all on these late night car rides. We tended to sit in friendly silence, listening to the songs on the radio. I wasn't sure why Bill had decided to speak up in this way now.

Bill's comment about Libby made me remember mule traders coming through our neighborhood when I was a child. They would walk their mules down the platform of their truck to show them to the farmers. It always made me feel sad to see how the owners of the mules jerked the creatures around, turning them about and discussing their good qualities, as if they only thought of the animals as property. I wanted Daddy to buy them so they wouldn't have to go through that misery anymore.

"I don't want to ever again go to bed with anyone," I told Bill in the car that night.

Bill laughed. "You'll change your mind about that, I'm sure." He paused for a moment before adding, "You know, Dean, my friend Jack is really stuck on you. I'm glad you're so nice to him. He's very rich, did you know that? His family is one of the wealthiest families in America."

In spite of my happiness on those dates with Jack, it started to become clearer to me how dangerous the bar was. One late summer evening, out of the blue, a bullet whizzed by me, a few inches above my head.

"You Goddamn whore hound, you leave my wife alone!"

The rifle bullet had been aimed at Bill's head, as I soon found out. Bill had been standing behind the bar helping Jesse. I quickly lay my head down on the bar, in the midst of people screaming, and I was afraid to lift it, while the police rushed in to arrest the shooter, so I didn't see who he was.

We closed the bar early that night and Jesse took me home, because the officers were questioning Bill.

As he drove, Jesse said, "Whew! That was a close shave for you and Bill and me. You don't look as shook up as I feel, though."

I croaked a response. "I'm still in shock."

"I knew Bill was going to get in trouble, seeing so much of that guy's wife. She's been in there hanging around Bill a lot lately. You've seen her."

I thought about that. I had noticed a woman who wore nice clothes and flung her long black hair over her shoulder so that it cascaded down her back. She looked like a model.

"I didn't know. I thought she was Bill's wife."

Jesse laughed. "Not a chance."

"But I heard Bill tell the police he was innocent, and that it was a case of mistaken identity."

"Oh, yeah, sure," he softly said, with a touch of sarcasm.

I felt grateful to be alive, but that night I tossed in my bed, thinking about what could have happened to me. What would my family have thought, if they'd heard I'd been injured by gunfire in a bar in Miami? By dawn, I had made up my mind that after the next paycheck I would quit that job.

The following night, however, Jack came to sit with me again. He saw me almost each night that week, in fact, and each time his tip was so large – two hundred dollars, sometimes more – that he would be the only person I had to "entertain" the entire evening.

Bill's words, "Jack is really stuck on you," kept playing over in my mind. The more I heard the words repeating inside me, the more elated I felt. I knew that I was hoping for a Cinderella story, as in a romantic movie, and that stories like that were pure fiction, yet I couldn't help imagining a happy ending to my story with Jack. He certainly seemed to be as fond of me as I was of him. Why would he bother to pretend something he didn't feel?

I continued to work at the bar into the early fall, and I held onto my hopes about Jack, in spite of the fact that he had not yet mentioned marriage. I often wonder what would have happened if events hadn't woken me up with a sharpness I could not have foreseen.

On the night of October 14, 1955 -- a night I will never forget -- I took a seat on a barstool beside Libby, as I often did at the beginning of the evening, before the customers started to come in. I hoped Jack would come that night. I hadn't seen him for over a week.

As I sat next to Libby, Bill's crude remark about her came to my mind again and made me sad, but I was even sadder seeing her, at the beginning of our shift, drinking a straight bourbon, with change from her twenty dollar bill beside her glass.

Thinking she seemed as lonely as I was, I started a conversation.

"You know, I think I'm falling in love with Jack," I said, "because I find myself thinking about him all during the day at the office. Do you know if he's married?"

Libby took a long, hard stare at me as her chin dropped. Looking around carefully, to make sure no one was near enough to hear, she moved her stool closer to me. Then she placed her arm around my shoulder and said, "Baby Face, you don't fall in love with anyone in this business."

"Why?"

She whispered in my ear. "Ignoring the fact that Jack is married and has two young'uns, he happens to be more dangerous than most. He is a big shot in the Mafia and his dad is an even bigger big shot."

"What is the Mafia?" I asked, thinking of what Bill had told me about how rich Jack was. "I heard Jack comes from one of the wealthiest families in America."

"Yes, he does. The Mafia is the biggest crime syndicate in the world. They refer to themselves as The Family."

All my dreams about Jack slipped away and melted in that instant. I looked at Bill with total disgust and knew without a doubt that I would leave the bar. Cast onto my own resources once more, I would have to find another extra job.

Soon the after-dinner drinkers started to drift in. Usually a raft of heavy drinkers arrived around 8:00 and drank beer steadily, sometimes with bourbons in between, until about 10:00, and then perhaps they would greedily swallow a hamburger or a bowl of chili with their last beer in an effort to be sober enough to drive home.

Jack did not show up that night. Looking across the bar around 9:00, I noticed Libby's limber body drooping to the point of nearly falling off her stool. I had noticed she had been drinking heavily since our conversation, and according to the schedule in the kitchen she had not taken a lunch break. The man who had been sitting with her had bought her a beer each time he had one. Within an hour, she had drunk four beers in a row.

I saw Bill noticing Libby, and I expected he would call her away to have her lunch break, as he usually did in such cases, but he didn't seem to care. Remembering his conversation about her, I guessed maybe he really didn't care. After all, she was selling beer to her date and that meant more profit for Bill.

Her drinking partner was not a regular, and as I looked at him more closely, I realized that he looked like one of the roughest men I had ever seen. His bushy brown hair was in tangled knots as if it had not been brushed for days, and his reddish beard had a dark crusty patch that I thought might be dried, dirty blood.

Soon Libby and this strange customer staggered together out the back door. It was clear they were going up to one of the bedrooms.

About half an hour later, I heard Libby's blood-curdling screams and thuds of flesh being pounded on.

A coarse voice shouted, "Goddamn that bloody bitch, she stole my money."

Now more flesh-pounding and more chilling screams from Libby.

Bill rushed toward the back, calling over his shoulder, "Jesse, call the police!"

Bill and Ed, a kitchen worker, carried Libby into the bar area, where I stood trying to stay out of the way. In a few moments, the police rushed through the front door, almost colliding with customers trying to get out.

I caught a never-to-be-forgotten last look at my friend Libby's face, dripping with blood. Her crushed eyes caught mine with a flickering of pain and hopelessness and a hard stare as she shook her head. I had the sense that she was trying to tell me, "Go back home to the farm where you're safe, before it's too late."

Moments later, without telling anyone, I grabbed my bag and coat, and rushed across the Venetian Causeway to the bus stop – never to return again.

Reaching my boarding house, I saw Stella sitting on the couch in the living room. Patting the cushion beside her, she said, "Sit down a few minutes, Dean, I want to chat with you."

I sat beside her, hoping she could not see how distressed I felt. Wryly, I thought about what a good actress I had proven myself to be, each night in the bar. In an effort to steady my mind, I looked up at the chandelier, remembering pleasant evenings I had enjoyed here in the boarding house with my friends. I couldn't forget Libby's news about Jack, though, or her screams and bloodied, bruised face. I felt that my happy life here in Miami Beach had been shattered.

Stella placed a hand on my arm as she said, "In two weeks my daughter and her husband will be returning and I'll be moving back to my home in Sarasota. I will miss you."

Tears stung my eyes. I felt bewildered by what had happened in the bar, and now Stella – who had been such a reassuring presence for me – wouldn't be here to greet me each night when I came home, or to give me breakfast each morning.

"Oh, I'm really going to miss you," I said, trying not to cry. "You have been so kind to me, Stella, and you know, you do remind me of my Grandma."

Stella coughed as she glanced out the window and then let her eyes rest on me with a worried expression. She looked as if there was something else she wanted to say, but she thought it best to keep quiet.

After a moment, she said, "Dean, I have been aware of the comfort you may have had, comparing me to your Grandma, and I have been flattered by that. I will leave my address and telephone number and hope you will call, and come and visit me. Also, I hope you have a pleasant relationship with my daughter Charlotte." Stella shook her head and the worried look came into her face again. "Unfortunately, after going through three marriages, Charlotte has had a hard time stabilizing her life, but I am hopeful she's more mature now."

If I had only had the wisdom to take a hint, I would have understood that Stella was warning me to be watchful and take care of myself, in relation to her daughter, who would now be collecting my rent.

Soon we embraced, and then I made my way down my lonely dark maze of crooks and turns until I reached my room. Quickly undressing, I tossed and turned in bed, trying to shed thoughts of the horror I had just witnessed. I kept hearing the sounds of Libby being punched, and her frightened cries for help. I kept seeing her injured eyes, and the blood on her face, as she stared at me.

Upon awakening, on the morning of October 15th, I felt relieved to be free of the bar job, yet quickly I had a daunting realization: without that extra job, I would no longer have sufficient income to send money home.

A few minutes before my alarm was set to ring, I heard a light knock on my door and Stella's voice.

"You have a long distance call from Georgia, Dean. Your brother-in-law Charles is on the phone."

My heart seemed to flip inside my chest. Charles on the phone? He never called just to talk. He must be calling with news I would be frightened to hear. How much more could happen in the world? As I pulled on my clothes under the bare light bulb of my room, I thought about poor Libby, my Mommy and Daddy, my Grandma, Colleen, and Gene. My whole life seemed to be poised to crumble and fall down about my ears.

4: Grandma

As I ran upstairs, I felt overwhelmed with foreboding, and my heart sank lower and lower with each breath. What could that phone call mean? On the first floor, I grabbed the receiver lying on a table in the living room.

"Odean, this is Charles. . . . Are you alone?"

His trembling voice sounded like someone else's.

Looking around desperately, I saw Tom and Stella in their chairs. Instantly sensing something was wrong, Stella rushed to turn off the television, as Tom dropped his newspaper to the floor and came over to stand beside me.

"No, my friends are here," I said to Charles, trying to sound normal.

"I have bad news."

I waited, not feeling able to ask Charles anything.

"Grandma Lawing died last night."

At first I could not comprehend his words. For a few seconds, I could not speak. When my voice came, it sounded like a wailing cry.

"What happened?"

"A heart attack. She just smothered, your Mommy and Daddy say, and there wasn't anything they could do to help her."

The receiver fell from my hand. Tom retrieved it, and Stella placed her arm around my shoulders.

Tom spoke into the phone, "Hello, Charles, this is Tom Galloway. I live in the boarding house with Dean. Please give me your number. We'll take care of Dean and call you right back."

As soon as Tom hung up, I said to my friends, as I sobbed, "I must go home. I have to go today. It's my Grandma."

That entire morning remains a blur in my mind, although a feeling of gratitude for those two friends has remained vivid in my heart. As I discovered after a few hours, Stella and Tom had taken care of my packing, the reservation of an airline ticket, and a call to my boss at the insurance company.

Midday, my sister Colleen called and we grieved together. Since I had left home, Colleen's and my correspondence had been only a few greeting cards. Now our hearts were meshed together in our shared sorrow.

After our tearful conversation, Colleen said, "Odean, here is Mommy."

I cried as I spoke first to Mommy and then to Daddy. Before I hung up, Mommy came on the phone again and asked if I could come home, and stay as long as possible. I knew my family had need of me.

"Yes, yes, Mommy. I will stay home with you until after Christmas."

By mid-afternoon, Tom and Stella had me ready to go to the airport. Before Tom took me in his car, though, I wanted to plan for my return. I remembered my arrival in Miami, two years earlier, and the difficulty that would have been insurmountable without the help of those lovely people at the bus station and then Stella. I wanted to make sure that when I came back to this boarding house in Miami Beach, I would be assured of my room.

I had taken quick note of my finances. From my bar salary, I had accumulated about seven hundred dollars, which I had removed from the shoebox under my bed earlier that morning and slipped into my billfold, along with the $200 that I had planned to send home as my usual monthly money order. Now, instead of purchasing that money order, I decided it would be best to hold onto the $200, and to give Stella whatever money would be necessary to cover the rent on my room for the upcoming ten weeks and more. A thought came to mind that I should be grateful for that bar, which had enabled me to have money for this emergency, but I couldn't quite feel grateful for the bar just yet.

"Tom," I said, "I would so appreciate your help with something, before I go."

"I'm glad to help you with anything," he said.

"When I was talking with my mother today, I promised her I would stay home with the family until after Christmas. I would be grateful if you could help me figure out how much cash I would

69

need to leave with Stella to secure my room until I return, after a period of staying home ten weeks."

"O. K. Let's go outside to our sitting area, because I think you could do with some fresh air."

Coming from the kitchen, where she had been preparing dinner, Stella said she had heard us talking about the rent.

"After you kids get Dean's finances figured out," she said, "please call me. I will bring my knitting out, and we might all sit together a bit before Dean has to leave us."

"Oh, Stella, please join us now," I said. "Our talk concerns you as well, since it's about how much I need to secure my room."

Stella agreed, and after each of us had settled into our favorite chairs on the small outside terrace, I said, "Stella and Tom, please accept my heartfelt gratitude for all your loving help in preparing me for this trip. I could not have gotten myself ready without you."

"Tom took care of most details," Stella said. "He went to the airport and got your reservation, and also your return ticket."

"Glad to do it," Tom said, as he shoved his hair back from his eyes, sweeping it over the top of his head.

Sitting in our cozy and comfortable seating area, I thought how pleasant the view was, although mainly we could see only the nice new apartment building towering above us. I thought about what a happy time I had had in this boarding house, and how nourished I had been by Stella's good meals and by our relaxed conversations right on this spot, warmed by the sun and refreshed by the sea breezes of Miami Beach. I remembered how we had celebrated together when Tom, who had been a chain smoker, had successfully given up cigarettes. Enjoying these memories, I felt a sense of comfort come over me.

"Are you sure it's necessary to leave all this money for future rent here with me at this time?" said Stella. "You could send the money later by mail."

"Oh, you don't understand," I said. "If I go home with any money, I will surely spend it all there, buying things for my family."

Tom calculated that $700.00 would cover ten weeks, plus an extra two weeks in January. I carefully counted out the $700.00, but by now my fingers were trembling so much that Stella patted my shoulder and reached for my hand to help me stuff the money inside an envelope Tom had given me.

"Dear Dean," she assured me, "your room will be waiting for your return and so will all your friends, and I am going to miss you when I have to leave here and go back to my own home."

Both she and Tom still looked as if they didn't understand why I was so insistent about this issue of advance payment, but Tom closed my cash record book and handed it back to me, seeming to feel it best not to pursue the subject and possibly cause any more stress for me that day.

"Thank you," I said to them both, and soon I hugged Stella goodbye, and gratefully jumped into Tom's car for the drive to the airport.

Once I was settled inside the Eastern Airlines plane, I knew Grandma would want me to feel a sense of excitement with the adventure of this, my first flight. Instead, the impact of Grandma's death sank more fully into my mind and heart, and I burst into tears before we had even taken off. I was glad the plane had only a few passengers. No one sat near me, possibly because of my crying, or maybe because they thought that I would like to be alone. Two people smiled sympathetically as they walked up the aisle.

I realized, as I sat in the airplane, looking out the window through blurry eyes, that the hardest blow I had ever experienced was this one, of facing the fact that I would never have the chance to give my Grandma a better life, as I had always dreamed I would do. Grandma's sweet smiling face kept flashing before my eyes, with scenes from one now sacred event after another. I remembered waiting for Mommy and Daddy to finish working in Mrs. Leach's garden, as I dressed Grandma in my imagination in the fancy clothes Mrs. Leach wore. I had always dreamt of the time when I could make enough money to buy Grandma and Mommy such nice clothes. I also remembered how, on my first day in Miami, when I saw the ocean for the first time, I felt that I could hear Grandma's voice, just as I had in my childhood, when I waded with her and Colleen in the small stream near our house. I pictured her tired face,

72

which broke into a smile as she said, "This little spring branch you kids are wading in as it passes, it will flow down this mountain and continue its journey, and after a while it will go right into the ocean, just like in the pictures we've looked at together. Oh, how I would love to see that ocean."

Now that dream of my Grandma seeing the ocean had been shattered with her passing, and I cried out in pain, knowing it would never become a reality.

Arriving in Atlanta, I followed the directions Charles had given me to the baggage collection area. I caught sight of him almost immediately.

"It's been a long time," he said, giving me a quick, shy hug.

As we drove along Northside Drive, heading to Highway 5, I recalled that Sunday evening, after my marriage, when Johnny and I had driven along this same route into Atlanta, and I had soon been shocked to learn that his "nice little apartment" was one musty, tiny room in the Atlanta slums, with the bathroom at the end of the hall. That day felt as if it had happened twenty years earlier, and not just four.

As I tried to talk with Charles, I realized that we felt uncomfortable with each other, and our words were sparse. Charles had never been wholly at ease in my presence, either before or after his marriage to Colleen. I had often sensed that he had accepted the general opinion of neighbors that Colleen's sister Dean was a bit strange. I imagined he felt fortunate that he had married the more settled Warren girl. My escape from my own marriage and my new life in Miami, so far from Georgia, may have made an even greater breach in our relationship. Charles tried valiantly to talk with me, though, and I did feel glad to see him.

Three hours later, we were making a right turn past our old familiar mailbox and easing up the dirt road. As we rounded the top of the hill, my eyes once again saw home, and I felt the enormous sense of joy and love for my family that had buoyed and sustained me all my life. Knowing, however, that Grandma would not be coming out to greet me, wiping her hands on her apron and ready to pull me into a big, warm hug, I felt the tears coming again. She would now be silent as she lay in her casket, a situation that seemed too painful for me to live through. Quickly, I reminded myself that my family needed me to be strong. Grandma would expect better behavior from me than to be hysterical and out of control.

The yard was filled with neighbors expressing their sympathy. The pained expressions on their faces made me feel even more distressed, because I knew they expected me to speak some words about the pleasure of seeing them again and the comfort of their presence at this time, but none of those nice words came from my mouth.

As I made my way through the crowd, I saw my parents standing on the porch, and I rushed to hug them.

"Mommy, Daddy," I cried, melting into their arms.

None of the hardships and disappointments I had seen them handle over the years had ever compared to this sad, sad loss. As I hugged Daddy, I felt how much thinner and older he was. Mommy was shaking so much that I wanted to give her some of my strength, or at least lead her to a chair, but that moment passed, as some more neighbors arrived with bowls of food.

Finding a path through the neighbors inside the house, I saw Grandma's open casket, but knew I could not yet look at her lifeless body. Instead, I walked as quickly as I could through the jam-packed hallway and onto the back porch, heading straight to Mr. Hagan's soft stuffed chair, which Grandma had inherited after his passing. There I sat, where the voices were drowned out by the sound of night birds and the gurgling of the creek in the background as it flowed over the rocks, making small, gentle waterfalls. I looked out on the huge white and red dahlias at the edge of the porch, which Mr. Hagan and Grandma had so carefully tended for years. Outwardly, it seemed that nothing had changed, but inside my heart all was different without Grandma animating this home with precious life.

After some time, Colleen came out to me and said, "Odean, you must come in and show your appreciation for the kindness of the neighbors."

"I will when I feel a little better," I said. "Right now, I am very angry at God for taking Grandma away from us."

"No, no, no, don't say that. It's blasphemous."

She turned to go back into the kitchen, leaving the screen door to slam behind her.

The three-day period of the wake seemed infinite, filled with a sense of stunned disbelief. On the morning of Grandma's burial, once the undertaker and neighbors had rolled her casket into the hearse, I followed inside and sat beside her body as the hearse moved slowly to the church. With my heart bursting with love, I talked to her and cried my gratitude in the silence. Even though I knew she could not hear me, I felt better.

In the little country church overflowing with neighbors and friends, the preacher's words beautifully expressed the goodness of Miss Ethie's life. However, even on this day, the preacher could not let go of the one fact that had plagued my Grandma all her life.

As he put it, "Miss Ethie's life was not without sin, but she got forgiveness and lived her later life as a prime example of a good Christian."

I squirmed in my seat as I felt an urge to rush to the pulpit, grab that preacher's blue and white tie, which hung so carelessly around his neck, and pull it until he choked. I knew the same story about Grandma that all the younger generations sitting there had received from their elders: "Miss Ethie is a good woman, but she had a bastard." Many of the neighbors would never forget a person's mistakes and often used such instances, years later, as examples for the young to learn valuable lessons.

Once the neighbors had shoveled the clay dirt back into Grandma's grave, they stayed for the customary goodbye words with my family, who talked with them and thanked them for their sympathy and help. I did not stay, however, but instead took off and ran to a little corner of the woods beside the cemetery, where Grandma had often taken me during church services, when I would get disturbed listening to the plaintive cries and pleas for Jesus to save the sinners. Many times when I was about five or six years old, I would whisper into Grandma's ear, as we sat on a bench inside the church, "Please take me away from these awful squalls." She would then take my hand and lead me into the woods, until their prayerful cries were a distant echo.

Colleen and Charles returned home to Rome, Georgia, soon after Grandma's burial. During the entire ten weeks I remained home with my parents and my brother Gene, we spent most of our time comforting each other. Once Christmas came, we treated it as if it were just an ordinary day. Without Grandma there to prepare food and celebrate with her beloved family members, it was no holiday to us.

Almost daily during my stay, I tried not to hear Mommy and Daddy's frequent plea, "Can't you stay just a few weeks longer?" Although I couldn't imagine leaving for Miami Beach again, I also knew I could not stay happily in Ellijay.

Some of the most difficult hours of those weeks were the occasions I spent in conversation with most all the neighbors who came by. During those visits, they never failed to ask me about my life as a model in Miami. I explained to them that my type of modeling at a wholesale dress manufacturer was not in the same category as the glamorous high fashion models people might see on the cover of *Vogue*.

Then to make myself feel a little better, I generally wove into my response something like this: "What's happening in my life that is most interesting is my acting lessons. I've become quite good at acting."

Remembering my intense effort to pretend to enjoy my conversations with the bar customers, I felt I could add a ring of truth to my voice as I spoke about my blossoming acting career. My bending of the truth seemed harmless enough to me at the time.

In spite of my parents' urgent pleas, I kept my promise to myself and prepared to leave. The three-hour drive with Mommy and Daddy felt wrenching, as they took me to the train station in their pick-up truck. Even though my ticket was to fly, I had told my parents I was going by train, so as not to worry them, since they were so afraid of flying. I was planning to take a taxi to the airport.

Hours later, as my flight was approaching Miami, the clunking sound of the airplane's wheels descending in preparation for landing disconcerted me, but not enough to hinder my joy as I looked out the window and saw the blue stretch of endless ocean. I consoled myself with the thought that I would soon be kicking that warm soft sand on the beach while the cheerful sun would be awakening my senses and bringing me peace. I marveled, in fact, at the sense of composure that started to envelope me now, as I accepted the fact that Grandma and I would never enjoy any more times together. I began to feel a revelation going on inside me. I felt sure that my fresh strength was a sign that Grandma had imparted to me her incredible ability to endure hardships and disappointments without flinching.

Thinking back to the painful goodbye with my parents several hours earlier in Atlanta, I realized Grandma's influence there as well, for I felt sure she had infused me with her own bravery, so that I had not caved in to my parents' pitiful pleadings of "Please stay just one more week."

"No," I said, with uncharacteristic firmness. "I have my ticket and the promise of my job waiting. I am very lucky that my boss held my job for me, these past ten weeks."

"I know," Mommy said, "but it's just that we love you so much and want to be with you every day."

I hugged her, both our hearts pressed together as we experienced another goodbye. I realized how much I had grown up, since I was able to say goodbye in person this time, and not in a letter.

"Mommy's right," said Daddy, "and we can't let our love for you hamper your life any longer. You have always been such a devoted and caring child."

"And I always will be."

I grabbed him into my arms and hugged him with all my heart. Pulling myself away, I waved, and as soon as they were out of sight, I grabbed a cab and headed to the Atlanta Airport, feeling a freedom that is known only to a caged bird taking flight.

5: Homeless

I was delighted to see Tom awaiting my arrival as I walked from the plane into the Miami airport. He greeted me with a smile and a hug.

"It's great to see you, Dean. I missed you and I've thought a lot about you, and how sorry I was you had to go home for such a sad occasion."

"Thank you, Tom," I said, as we started to walk to the baggage claim area. "I often thought of you and my Miami family at the boarding house, and I felt so grateful, knowing I would have you and my home here when I returned. That was a great comfort during these past weeks."

Tom nodded as he cast a quick glance my way, and just as quickly lifted his gaze to stare straight ahead. I thought I saw an uncomfortable expression flicker over his face, but he turned away so fast I couldn't tell for sure. At the baggage claim, he seemed unusually preoccupied with the process of retrieving my old brown suitcase from the table, where it had arrived with other bags. As he pulled it down for me, I noticed Johnny's Army dog tags, still attached to the handle. I made a note to myself to remove them before I traveled again.

As we approached the glass exit doors, I noticed a clock on the wall above them.

"Tom! It's 10:15 and you work tomorrow. You'll be late getting to bed. I have another day before I have to go to work."

"Don't worry, Dean. I'll be fine, and of course I wouldn't let you take a bus to the house."

I wondered why he looked away again, and why his voice trailed off -- that well-trained, clear voice that had served Tom well when he had been a disc jockey in Michigan. I wondered if something had happened with our boarding house, and I tried to remember what Stella had said about her daughter Charlotte coming to manage the house, once Stella had moved to Sarasota. Now it would be Charlotte who had the $700 I had given to Stella in advance. I shrugged this worry off, though, as I told myself that I was just imagining a change in Tom. Maybe he was simply tired or recovering from a cold, and didn't feel like talking. I reassured myself that I was just feeling vulnerable after a heart-rending day of goodbyes with my family.

I walked with Tom through the rain to the parking lot and hopped into his convertible, which had the top down.

As he started to drive, I said, "Tom, is everything alright?"

He smiled and spoke very gently. "Dean, you are uniquely intuitive. Or maybe my actions are more telling than I am aware. The truth is: all is not well at the boarding house."

I felt as if a swarm of bees had started up in my mind.

82

"Oh, what happened?"

So tired from the turmoil of emotions recently, I now began wondering whether some of the horror of my last night at the bar had somehow spilled over into my private life, perhaps some investigation into a murder.

I was preparing for something like that when Tom continued, "Do you remember how Charlotte was going to come live at the boarding house, and take over from her mother?"

I nodded. "I know it was Charlotte who was actually leasing the house," I said. "Stella had just been helping her out."

"Well, I hate to have to tell you this, but last week, Charlotte and her husband left town in the middle of the night with all the rent and board money we'd paid in advance." Tom looked at me sadly. "I know you gave a considerable amount of money to Stella in order to keep your room until you returned." He waited a few seconds, as if he was trying to get up his courage, before adding, "I'm afraid you lost all of that, Dean."

I was so stunned that I could barely comprehend what Tom was saying. Trying to compose myself, I asked, "How did all this happen?"

I could not bear to think our home had been uprooted, and our fellow boarders scattered. I had enjoyed the comfort of my friendships at our boarding house, and Stella's kindness. I could just picture how we had all sat together at breakfast, or after dinner, talking and laughing in our secure perch near the ocean. It came back to me now, how Stella had told me that Charlotte had gone through three marriages, and had had a hard time, although Stella had also said she thought her daughter was more mature now. Stella surely had been trying to warn me, if only I could have listened.

"I was in Key West," Tom was saying, "with my brother and his family -- they've been visiting from Michigan. Apparently Mrs. Kahn, the owner of the boarding house, came by last week and told everyone of the bad situation with Charlotte. The others already knew that Charlotte had taken the good silverware and some valuable furniture from the living room – remember that coffee table?"

I nodded, feeling stricken.

"Well, she'd gone off with that, and the good rocking chair, and whatever she could stuff in her car that night, I gather. That's why Diana and Mildred had called Mrs. Kahn, and when she came to talk to everyone, she told them that Stella's daughter had taken the rent money too. She also let them know that the power had been cut off, because Charlotte hadn't paid the bills for a couple of months. So Mrs. Kahn said, 'You renters no longer have lights or water in the house, but if you need to sleep here for the next two weeks while you find places to live, feel free to do so.' She gave us a grace period of two weeks, and she also set the date for the new tenants for a week or so after that. She said she'd need to have the cleaners come in, and to do a few repairs. It sounds as if she's going to raise the rent considerably." Tom sighed. "So I came back to this shambles. I was worried that Charlotte might have taken other things too, but thank heavens all she took from us renters was our advance rent payments."

I felt a cry rising up in me, to think of that $700, flown out the window now like paper birds. I had no savings left.

"What are we going to do about a place to live?" I asked.

"Jonathan and Vincent found another boarding place in Miami, where they can continue to share a room. Diana is now sharing an apartment with a girlfriend, and Mildred moved back home to her family in Jacksonville."

"So that leaves only you and me," I said. I felt a huge sense of relief suddenly that I would not be alone. "I'm so glad you're still here, Tom."

He took a big breath. "Now, since you have said that, I feel I must tell you that at the end of this week, I'll be returning home to Detroit. My brother and his wife will be driving back home after vacationing here, and I've decided to go back with them. My mother hasn't been well since my father passed on some months ago, and I'm needed at home."

Tom looked upset, having to tell me this personal information about his family and his upcoming move. He clearly felt worried about leaving me in this mess.

As Tom eased his car into the alley driveway, and around to the backyard of the dark boarding house, I thought about how much Tom was doing for his family in Michigan, just as I was trying to do for mine in Georgia. In addition to helping support his ailing mother, he was paying alimony for a young daughter.

Tom turned off the car lights and put on the brake. He came around to open the door for me, as gentle and caring as ever, and as I stepped out under his umbrella, I managed to say, "I'll be lost without you, Tom, but I understand."

"Before we go inside," he said, "we'll have to go to the grocery store, because it's almost their closing time. There's no water in the house, so we have to use the bathroom there. That's what I've been doing."

He gently touched my elbow as we walked together under the umbrella, sharing quiet sympathy. I was too shocked to make any further conversation.

After our trip to the Publix grocery store nearby, I decided to stay in Diana's empty room on the second floor, rather than find my way down to my tiny bedroom in the dark. Since Diana had already moved, her bed had no sheets, so I lay down in my clothes and tried the best I could to get a little sleep.

The next morning, after going to the bathroom again at Publix, I pulled a wrinkled dress out of my suitcase, and tried to smooth it by hand, because there was no electricity for an iron. After Tom and I ate a little bread and jam, he drove me to work at the insurance company.

My co-workers were glad to have me back and expressed sympathy about my grandmother. As I sat at my desk, I felt a sense of stability in familiar surroundings. It occurred to me that this was the only home I now had. For the first time since moving to Miami, I realized how much I had missed, in not forming fuller friendships here with my co-workers. I keenly regretted my daily rushing out of this office to night work at the bar.

While at the office each day that week, I continued to comb the want ads of my boss's *Miami Herald* for a cheap room to rent. Tom did the same for me at his own office, searching the newspapers for an affordable room in a safe neighborhood. Each evening when he picked me up, we compared notes about any ads we had seen. Since the winter season was in full swing, however, most rooms had already been rented, and the few available rooms were too expensive.

One night, as Tom and I walked into the boarding house, I said, "I know I could go back to that bar, work there and have a room and meals, but I will not go there again."

Tom reached to hold my hand. "Bless your heart," he said. "You know, Dean, I have always felt protective of you, ever since you appeared on Stella's doorstep in the storm. None of us knew quite what to make of you that morning, this lonely little elf from Georgia. You've done well for yourself here, with your job at the insurance company, and I am so glad to hear you won't be going back to working in a bar."

Together we lit a couple of candles at the dining table and Tom brought out some bread and honey, and a little peanut butter.

Over the course of that week most all the groceries had spoiled, without a refrigerator. Tom's generosity touched me, and as we ate, I opened up for the first time about my experience in Bill's bar.

"I would rather die young and fast," I said, "than have to go through a slow death, like one of the girls I knew there." I told him the whole story about Libby, and I was grateful to Tom for his quiet compassion.

"Well, Dean," Tom said, "all I can say is, I am so very glad you left that bar. You don't have to go to a job like that. If you still need a second job, I know you can find a good one." He added, "I'll go grocery shopping for you before I leave."

"Oh no, no, you don't need to do that." The pride I had inherited from my dear mountaineer parents and my Grandma flew out of my mouth as I reached for a story -- really, a lie.

"The day you leave," I said, "I will be moving in with a girl I work with, and I'll stay with her and her family until I find a place."

Tom smiled as if the sun had just come out. "Dean, that is truly a relief for me to hear you have found a place."

My lie had made him feel better about me, and I felt a little better inside myself too, strengthened by knowing I was following a tradition of proudly making my own way -- "keeping my problems within the family," as my Daddy would say -- no matter what.

Realizing how worried my Mommy and Daddy would be should they call the boarding house and get a cut-off response, I wrote them to contact me at the insurance company. I told them that

88

I had moved and that my new room did not have a telephone in just yet. Now another lie had come out easily -- as easily as reaching for another hot dog at the old Varsity in Atlanta, where I had always been so hungry.

The day Tom's brother came to pick him up, Tom and I gave each other a hug and a promise that we would write to each other. Then I watched my only friend in Miami waving as he disappeared around the block, heading a distance of hundreds of miles. The two-week grace period would be up, as of the following morning, and Mrs. Kahn could come to claim the house any day now. I hoped she would wait at least one more week before the new tenants would move in, as she had promised, but I couldn't be sure.

Walking back toward the house, I decided that I should shampoo my hair later that day in the Publix bathroom, since I hadn't washed it in over a week. Because another storm had started, maybe it would just look to other shoppers as if I had been out in the rain. I panicked, though, that evening, as I started to walk down the slick, unlit driveway toward the grocery store. This was the first time I had used the store's bathroom alone. The previous nights, Tom had come with me, and being with someone in the same situation had helped.

As I walked in the rain, my breath began to come in short, strange gasps, and my head started to ache. I felt anxious that I might smother, just as my Grandma had, and die right on the driveway, in the storm. What if I became totally homeless? Georgia seemed so far away at that moment, and I felt like a cornflower, beaten down by the impersonal rain.

Somehow, once I had entered the bathroom, I managed to get a little better control of my trembling hands, as I put a small towel from the boarding house around my neck and picked up the lavatory bar of soap. I busied myself shampooing, trying just to focus on becoming clean. At that moment a lady wearing a mink stole came into the bathroom to wash her hands, the big diamond on her finger sparkling. Raising my head, I smiled at the rich lady, who immediately turned and ran out the door as if terrified of what I might do to her. In a hurry to get out, I rubbed my hair with the towel and then combed it quickly. Just outside the bathroom door, I hesitated, as I saw the lady signal one of the store workers, who wore an apron saying "Publix Grocery."

The lady asked, "Are you the manager?"

"Yes," the worker said.

"Well, there's a vagrant woman in the bathroom, washing her hair. She was staring at my jewelry and I felt very unsafe."

Heat suffusing my face, I swiftly passed them and ran into the alley leading back to the boarding house.

I had never heard the word "vagrant." Being curious about how I had appeared to the wealthy lady, I lit a candle in Diana's room and opened the little dictionary Mr. Hagan had given me. My shaking finger pointed to the definition of "vagrant": "A person, such as a drunkard, who constitutes a public nuisance."

I thought of the caring hands of Mr. Hagan, as he gave me the dictionary, and how sad he would be if he could see me now -- someone described as a public nuisance. I thought of my Grandma too, who was always ready to comfort me with a loving hug and a good word.

It was now, as I held the dictionary open to that new word, that I felt the full blow of my Grandma's death. As I thought about the weeks I had just spent with my family in Georgia, I realized that I had been constantly feeling Mommy's pain, ignoring my own sense of loneliness and sorrow as I tried to comfort her. Daddy too had frequently broken down weeping. With bitter words, he had often reprimanded himself for not getting Grandma immediately to a doctor when she began smothering on the morning of her death. Time after time, I had tried to comfort him, saying, "Daddy, please don't blame yourself. The doctor could not have done anything to keep Grandma from dying."

My Mommy had been so distraught about the sudden loss of her mother that I had often found her talking to Grandma in the most plaintive way, and I had constantly rushed to her side to hug her. She had kept Grandma's rocker piled high with clean laundry, saying, "It's so lonely to see her rocker empty."

After putting Mr. Hagan's dictionary on the table and blowing out the candle, I could not sleep. I was alone in the boarding house for the first time, the rain still flinging itself at the windows. It had been stormy just like this on my first day in Miami Beach, over two years earlier, yet I had felt protected then by Stella, and filled with enthusiasm, proud of having won my freedom to be on my own and hopeful about beginning some college courses one day. My heart had been bursting with happy daydreams, which now appeared to have flown out the window with my rent money.

The house's eerie, creaking sounds, mingling with the wind and rain rattling the windows, reminded me of rainy nights in my childhood, when my Grandma's arms had cuddled me in her warm, soft lap. Yet Grandma wasn't here. She wasn't anywhere on earth. I felt so sad and weak; I could not face getting out of bed and going back to Publix in the morning, or even walking to the bus stop. I began to fear that I would not be able to go to work at all, and the result would be a day's wages taken from my check. I worried too that even if I went to work, this house might be locked to me by the following afternoon when I tried to come home.

It was about three in the morning, after hours of wakefulness, when something enormous happened -- not outside, but inside my soul. Suddenly I felt as if something just broke, and I had a tremendous urge to give up.

At first I couldn't identify the new feeling welling up inside me. Then the realization struck me that this was despair. For the first time in my life, I no longer had hope. The one feeling that had kept me going through many bad times in my young life had now disappeared.

One by one, many raw and disappointing scenes began to play over in my mind. First, my foolish marriage with my drunken husband came crashing like broken glass into my mind. One of the most painful of all the emotional scenes from my marriage was the time when Johnny had lost his job, and I had had to put on hold once again my dream of college courses.

Next, I began to recall the frightening choices I had made at the end of my marriage. I pictured that Clark Gable look-alike, the preacher / car salesman, and our room in the Biltmore Hotel. I pictured the "doctor" and his icy cold instrument performing the agonizing illegal procedure as he held a cigarette hanging from his dry lower lip.

As the windows in Diana's room grew a bit lighter with the approach of dawn, I started to sense the arrival of a solution to all of this devastation. Maybe my life could be worth something, to my family at least. Maybe I would not have to worry anymore about finding a room in Miami and enough money to pay my rent.

I kept thinking about my childhood friend Glen. After he had been killed in action during the Battle of Normandy, his parents had received a government insurance check in the amount of $10,000, which was a huge amount of money in those days. With that amount, the Simpsons had bought a "beautiful rich black-dirt farm." Those were the words Daddy often used to describe John Henry

Simpson's new property. I could picture the bright expression on Daddy's face as he talked about his friend's brand new farm.

"Now John Henry is all set for life, tilling that rich soil," he would say.

I thought about how I would love to know that my Daddy could have that same happy look on his face one day soon, as he would talk about his own "beautiful rich black-dirt farm." Maybe he would be even happier than he was when I saved up to buy him his shiny new tractor.

As dawn lightened the windows, I worked out a plan. It filled me with joy, and I went to sleep for half an hour in a sweet, promising frame of mind.

Upon awakening, I rushed to the grocery store and skipped among the early shoppers on my way to the bathroom, no longer worried about ladies with diamond rings on their fingers. I no longer hung my head low in embarrassment, but proud and high. I was now embarked on a mission I knew would be successful. Once I was dressed and had eaten a few crackers left over from Tom's supply, I put the key under the mat, hoping that Mrs. Kahn would not retrieve it and take over the house that day.

Then I was off to the bus, headed for work at the insurance company. I had important details to take care of, as I began to follow my plan to its fulfillment.

6: From Deepest Despair to the White Cadillac

As the bus rumbled along MacArthur Causeway a few minutes later, I happily contemplated my mission of freedom from all the cares that beset my family and me. Physically, nothing had changed in my situation, but my thoughts about everything were fresh and purposeful on this bright morning in Miami. Like Glen, I was going to buy a substantial insurance policy, and arrange for my family to benefit from it.

Upon entering the office, I didn't madly rush to grab *The Miami Herald* from my boss's desk, to search the ads for a cheap room. I was no longer fretting about the very real possibility that I would soon be out on the street.

From the hallway outside our office came the familiar sound of Mr. Clarkson's smoker's cough. His private secretary Jennifer and I assumed he was plagued with that malady, since we had to empty his ashtray several times each day. In discussing our boss, Jennifer and I had agreed that his smoking habit was his only negative quality.

Mr. Clarkson entered the office, smiling as he coughed. "Good morning, Dean. I hope you've found a room. I think you said your grace period was up today?"

"Oh, thank you, Mr. Clarkson, I did find a room," I said.

"I'm so glad. We were all concerned for you, and I do hope it's a nice room near us, so you won't have such a long commute."

I didn't answer, but asked him a question instead. "Mr. Clarkson, would you ask your friend who sells life insurance if I might have an appointment to talk to him about me buying a policy?"

As if my question were the most ordinary one in the world, he said cheerfully, "Yes, I'll be glad to do that. I'll be seeing him at lunch today."

I knew that if he had been able to see into my mind, his cheerfulness would have turned into worry for me. I kept up my smiles, though, and Mr. Clarkson clearly felt that all was well.

That afternoon I signed a policy for $10,000 of life insurance with Mr. Forbes. The contract was scheduled to be completed and go into effect one week later. Since I would need to make a payment on the policy, I realized I couldn't send any money home from the first paycheck I had received since returning from Georgia. Although this realization bothered me, I now trusted that my family's immediate lack would be overcome shortly. With great relief, I considered how that insurance policy would allow me to leave this world with a comfortable sense of knowing that my Mommy and Daddy would be taken care of after I died, and that was all that really mattered.

After work, as my bus went east again, back over the Causeway to Miami Beach, I smiled, remembering my first trip home from work in Tom's convertible. With breezes caressing my face, I had gazed at the ocean glittering ahead, and the graceful hotels of Miami Beach, and then, looking in the side view mirror, I had seen my ponytail dancing wildly in the wind. That had been the most carefree moment of my life since early childhood. All in a short time, I had found a place to live near the ocean, a good job, and also the pleasure of my new friendship with this calm, good person. I had been full of hope and secure in the thought that my good luck would continue. Feeling ready to explore and find my niche in that exciting new territory of Miami, I had mused that Ponce de Leon must have felt the same rush of excitement when he'd discovered that glorious tip of the United States.

Now, over two years later, I looked at Miami Beach without seeing the magnificent hotels. They no longer held any magic for me. My hope of living a happy life of plenty in a hotel like those, or in a mansion like Mrs. Leach's, had disappeared. I missed the bright dreams I had always cherished, yet I was glad to know I would soon have no more tired, unhappy and worrisome days. The sweet confidence that the insurance policy would make a difference in the lives of my parents was the one dream I still had.

Looking out the bus window at the endless blue ocean, I whispered softly, "Grandma, soon Mommy and Daddy will have money to buy rich, fertile acres of bottom farmland. I'll tell you about it when I see you in heaven."

I liked thinking that I could soon be talking to Grandma like that, although I didn't really believe it would be possible. Even if conversing with Grandma should happen, I envisioned that she would see the truth of my actions, and her response, strongly put but with gentle words, might be something like this: *My dear little girl, what in God's name were you thinking? You must understand that using the insurance policy for your family's benefit was actually stealing and was a sin.* For sure, she would tell me how horrible it would be for my parents if they were to find out I had taken my own life in order to give them a better one. In spite of knowing how Grandma would point out those facts, however, I was so set on what I felt was best to do, that I ignored the wise and ethical path I knew she would urge, if she could.

Exiting at my bus stop, I rushed to the porch, comforted to find the house key still in the spot where I had placed it earlier in the day. Mrs. Kahn had not taken over the house yet. I felt grateful to her, and thought maybe, just maybe, nothing about the house would change until my insurance policy became effective in just a few more days. Even if she sent in some housecleaners, or carpenters for the repairs, possibly I could continue to live in Diana's room without attracting any notice.

I hurriedly ate a tin of sardines, some crackers and a can of peas, without tasting any of it, and then I drank a glass of water. I knew I would need food to give me strength, because I intended to walk to the beach to rehearse my plan. Before going to the ocean, I would need to get to a bathroom and do my laundry and bathroom chores.

I had discovered a smaller grocery store a few blocks further down Abbot Avenue, which had an outside back entrance to the bathroom. I gathered my laundry into a basket and headed toward this market. Luckily, I was able to wash my clothes and myself without anyone paying attention to me. After brushing my teeth, I placed my freshly washed laundry in my basket and walked outside. I quickly dropped off the laundry at the boarding house, and then began walking toward the beach, as the sunset started to fade. Once there, I went to my usual spot, on a quiet stretch of sand, with no people in sight.

As I sat on the sand, I considered the fact that tomorrow I had to call Mr. Forbes and remind him of how important it was that he mail my policy to my Daddy at Route 2, Ellijay, Georgia, and then call me at the office to let me know what day he had mailed it, and when the policy would become active. I wanted to make double sure of his promise to do all this. I could not let my mind become foggy. I was anxious that I would miss taking care of one of the items I needed to get done before I took my walk straight into those waves.

I felt surprised by the way in which the soft crashing of the waves soothed me. Reassuring myself that my decision was a good one and quite simple, I pictured how I would leave my shoes on the beach, and then walk slowly ahead into the water, in my bare feet, with just a light dress on, and keep walking, as the water came up to my calves, and then my knees, and then my hips. I would walk until the water reached my neck, and went over my head. I knew I wasn't a strong swimmer, and I was sure that, even if I tried to swim, I would not be able to stay afloat for long. I figured that it would not take very long to drown, and then I would be out of the world entirely.

After half an hour of these images and thoughts, I stood up, brushed the sand from my clothes and glanced north; toward where I knew Palm Beach must be, about seventy miles away. I remembered the soft summer evening when Mrs. Leach had spoken to my parents about adopting me and bringing me each winter to her house in Palm Beach. She had said that I "exuded enthusiasm."

There it was again – that word "enthusiasm" – just as in my favorite quote from Ralph Waldo Emerson, the one Mr. Hagan had given to me on a framed poster: *Nothing great was ever achieved without enthusiasm.* As I stood on the sand, my mind hungrily latched onto joyful memories of those years when Mr. Hagan had been so encouraging. I remembered sitting with him, both of us reading quietly together, or talking about what we had read. I remembered how happy and proud he had been that I loved philosophy just as he did.

I remembered, too, the many precious happenings during all my growing-up years: eating my Grandma's rich biscuits and honey, helping Grandma and Mommy in the kitchen, hoeing in the fields with Colleen, walking over the hill to the mailbox, or walking with my Daddy along the path to the Andy Spring. I felt with a new and painful intensity how privileged I had been to spend so many days with my family and Mr. Hagan. It struck me with full force that it had been the moments of daily living that had made my young life so happy. As I stood on the sand, facing the ocean in front of me, I felt a growing understanding of that truth, and my heart kept overflowing with gratitude.

A panorama of more scenes of my childhood continued to float through my mind: Grandma handing me her fresh moon pies, or rubbing my back when I was tired; Mommy washing the clothes at the stream as she smiled and listened to me read *Gone With the Wind*; Daddy and me mashing the corn out in the woods, or sitting on the rocks beside the Andy Spring, watching the clear water making bubbles come up between the rocks, as we talked together. How good the spring water had tasted, as we had drunk from a gourd hanging on a nearby limb! In his contemplative moments, Daddy had liked to speak about God's earth; in such a way that I knew he believed God and Earth were inseparable, part of one great whole. I had always liked that about Daddy. His sense of the sacred in nature had reminded me of the American Indians, who had loved those mountains too, when they had made their homes there before we did.

Also pressing on my memory for entrance were many sweet scenes of my brother Gene as a baby and later as a growing boy.

Perhaps for the first time in my life, I felt total appreciation for Colleen and how hard she had tried to get me to be like everyone else. I could now see that her stern, bossy manner had demonstrated her special caring for my welfare, because she so wanted me to fit in.

As I turned from the beach and started to walk the few steps to Collins Avenue, my feeling of gratitude for my family increased so powerfully that my heart melted and tears ran down my face. I had to face the fact that, in carrying out my plan, I would never see my family again. I felt as if I was about to close a book – the book of my life – which I had been so privileged to live.

Without looking, I started jaywalking across Collins Avenue. So filled with my daydreams, I did not judge the speed of an approaching car, and in the next instant, as I tried to get out of the way, I fell to the cement, while the gigantic car skidded to a stop, a few feet from me. All I could hear was the piercing squeal of brakes, as the bright headlights on the massive chrome fender rushed toward me. A blow to my head from hitting the cement must have injured me, because I quickly realized that the wetness dripping into my eyes was blood. My head and leg felt tender and sore.

Remembering that it was illegal to jaywalk, I scrambled as best I could to the curb. Glancing back, I saw the face of the driver in the big white car, who looked as if he was just staring at me in a state of shock. As I swiped my eyes on my sleeve to clear the blood from them, I caught a glimpse of the car's New York license plate.

From the sidewalk, I limped into some shrubbery and fled back to the boarding house.

Grabbing a flashlight from the hall as I entered, I went into Diana's bedroom. Once I shone the flashlight on my leg, and saw blood, I rolled a towel around the cut, and slipped under the covers in the darkness, in case the police might be following me. I feared that the driver of that white Cadillac might have told police to look for my body in the bushes, and they might trace the trail of blood. It did not occur to me that the driver would be considered by the police to be the one at fault. I felt in the wrong, since I had not paid attention when crossing the street, and I was in this house illegally.

As I lay in bed, listening to the ocean in the distance, however, I started to grow more peaceful. I was at least glad it was Friday night and I would have two days to recover before going back to work. I started to remember the driver, how horrified he had looked. Maybe he had been worried about me. He hadn't really appeared to be someone who would have alerted the police. In the surprised instant in which I had caught a glimpse of his face, he had looked like a handsome man, clean-shaven and healthy. A kind man, maybe even as kind as Mr. Hagan.

A question began to shimmer in my thoughts, as I finally relaxed enough to grow sleepy. The question mingled with all the good memories I had had of my family and Mr. Hagan, right before the big white car had hit me: had that Cadillac been a white angel of death, or the magnificent steed of a new hero-rescuer?

103

7: The Day After

My eyes opened to see brilliant sun flooding the bedroom. Touching the skin just above my hairline and over my right eye, where I had hit the cement, I was thankful that, as best I could tell, my wound had started to heal. As I tried to roll over on the bed, though, the excruciating pain made me stop. At first I worried that I had broken my hip or even my back, yet I realized   after a few minutes that I was alright, if I could just move carefully and slowly.

Summoning all my courage, I brought my feet onto the floor beside the bed and removed the bloody towel from my leg. I was relieved to see that the cut was not as deep as I had thought. With nausea now mixing with pain, I lay slowly back on the bed and rested for another hour. I felt grateful for the cheerful sunshine, which continued to soothe my sore limbs, helping me trust that I would soon have greater freedom of movement.

As soon as I cautiously stood up, I could see severe blue bruises on my right hip. I realized it would be best to dress in long pants, to hide my leg wound. Slowly, I limped my way across the room to the closet, and managed to get dressed in a comfortable pair of pants. Thank heavens it was Saturday, and I would not have to dress for work! Walking along the two blocks to the grocery store was difficult, but once I reached the public bathroom, it was comforting to take a sponge bath in warm water. After bathing, I looked and felt better.

On my way back to the house, as I passed the popular restaurant Pumperniks, the smell of pastries and freshly brewed coffee made my mouth water. I had eaten so little in the two days since Tom had left. During the whole time I had lived in Miami Beach, I had passed Pumperniks almost daily, often glimpsing the well-dressed, carefree people inside, but I had never been as hungry and bereft as I felt that morning. In winters this restaurant was filled each day with wealthy, tanned men, and women dressed in short robes over bathing suits, wearing huge diamond rings on their fingers. The customers always looked relaxed and happy, whether the weather was rainy or sunshine spilled in from the huge glass windows. Most of the people, Tom had told me, were from New York or Canada, or other places that grew cold in winter. In passing the entrance, I had often overheard friends greeting each other, exclaiming, "It's 10 degrees back home today! Boy, are we lucky to be here now." Only the elite could afford these beautiful Miami Beach hotels, of course, especially in the winter season. In summer, I had discovered, the rates would be cut in half, although I knew how impossibly high they still would be for people like my Mommy and Daddy.

As I walked back from the market bathroom, I couldn't remember the last time I had felt even half as carefree as those privileged people at Pumperniks. I did feel blessed today, though,

106

that I hadn't been killed by that Cadillac. I passionately hoped I could stay alive for four more days, when my insurance policy would become effective.

I felt tempted to go around the building to the kitchen door of the restaurant and ask if they would please give me some stale pastries or just some pieces left on the customers' plates. Yet, as I remembered my Daddy and Mommy's absolute refusal to accept charity in any form for our family, I tried to ease my hunger pangs with sweet memories of my poor but proud heritage.

In the boarding house, I practically fell into the bed covers. I hoped Mrs. Kahn would not choose this day to come and take back the key. If she did, I planned to sleep that night in the safest spot I could think of – the cement area behind the house, where the garbage cans sat. At least that area was familiar, because I had seen it each day for so many months, through the tiny window in my basement room. I had been inside looking out, and now I would be outside looking in.

I no longer cared about food, even though I knew I should eat something. To get out of bed and look through the pantry in the kitchen seemed more than I could manage. During that entire morning and early afternoon, I alternated between the bed and a chair, trying to find one precious moment of relief. By mid-afternoon, I lapsed into a delirious state. In what seemed like a dream, I imagined myself to have become Mommy, as she was in my early childhood. As my Mommy, I was back in our two-room shack, crying with pain, just the way she cried when she had mastoiditis. I woke myself up with my sobs, and as I lay in bed, wiping away my tears, I thought about how angry I had gotten at God, when Mommy had been sick, because He would not give Mommy any relief. I didn't feel angry with God now, though. Instead, I felt I deserved this awful situation, after the way I had lived.

Once I calmed down, I finally dropped off into sound sleep, and when I awoke, the sun had started to set. Even with my sore head and legs, I felt drawn to the beach again. Hoping the ham Tom had bought had not totally spoiled, I made myself eat a piece of it, and I drank some water from a glass jar I always filled when I went to the store bathroom.

Outside, as I approached Abbott Avenue and started to turn right toward Collins Avenue, I happened to look up, and in that astonishing moment, I was surprised to see the same man who had almost run over me in his white Cadillac. He was standing on the opposite side of the street, staring at me with an equally surprised look on his face. I gathered that he had just jumped out of a long, shiny black car, where a man and a woman were still sitting in the front seat. He walked quickly toward me, and this time he was the one who was jaywalking!

As he reached me, he said, "Didn't I almost run you over a last night?"

"Yes," I said weakly.

He looked back across the street toward his companions, and called to them, "Please go ahead to the Fontainebleau. I'll join you there later."

The friend in the driver's seat smiled and waved. I thought he looked a lot like Milton Berle, one of the top television comedians in those days, but I didn't think that was possible.

The Cadillac owner turned to me and extended his hand. As I took it, my hand trembled at first touch, yet quickly I felt comforted by his warm friendly grasp.

"I am so glad to see you!" he said. "I was afraid my car had seriously injured you."

Tears came into his eyes as he placed his arm around my shoulder. I was stunned. I couldn't figure out what to make of his attitude. Why was he all that bothered about it? It must have looked to him as if I had deliberately lunged in front of his car. In the next instant, I had the wild thought that somehow he understood how desperately I wanted to live for four more days, until my insurance would become effective and I could walk into the ocean.

"Come, walk with me to my porch, and let's talk."

He pointed to a gate opening onto a complex of vine-covered villas nearly hidden from the street. I had often wondered about the impressive people who must inhabit the large, lovely hotels, yet I had completely ignored the low-lying villas, which were much less ostentatious. I could see now that these villas were quite pretty and welcoming.

As we walked toward his porch, he became aware that I was limping.

"You did get badly hurt, didn't you?"

Looking into his concerned eyes, I got my first full glimpse of his handsome features. To me, he looked the image of Prince Philip, Queen Elizabeth's husband, whom I had seen in photographs of her Coronation a few years earlier. Those photographs of the Queen and Prince Philip had shown him to be a tall, thin, graceful and athletic man with a big smile. Jerry was above average in height, and his athletic body looked similar to the prince's, even though Jerry was some years older. Ever since my teenage crush on Mr. Hagan, I had tended to find older men appealing, and Jerry's age made him that much more attractive to me, especially in combination with his aristocratic looks and great kindness.

Years later, when Sylvia and Ed Sullivan had become my good friends, I once mentioned the clear resemblance Jerry had with Prince Philip.

"Jerry is a real prince!" I said.

Ed flashed that big smile of his, and then threw back his head, laughing loudly.

"Did I hear you right?" he asked, still laughing. He bent closer to me and cupped his ear to hear me better.

I blushed and pretended he had indeed misheard me. This time I said, "I've hurt some since," hoping "since" sounded enough like "Prince." I don't think I fooled Ed, though, because he often enjoyed calling Jerry a prince, and winking at me.

Now this prince guided me toward the lit-up porch of his villa.

"Here, come, let's sit on my porch and talk," he said, as he helped me to sink into the softest lounge chair on which I had ever sat. As I smiled at this handsome man with the kind eyes and started to talk with him, my clear plan to drown myself in four days appeared to grow fuzzy and fade, as I felt my heart lighten.

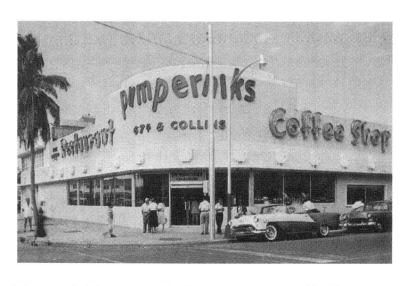

Figure 1: Pumperniks Restaurant on Collins Ave.

8: Breakfast at Pumperniks

I awakened in a dreamy state, in a big and comfortable bed, cocooned in fragrant, fresh sheets. The villa was hushed and quiet, because I had slept in it on my own, while the villa's owner slept at his brother's home in Coral Gables. The bed seemed to float in rich darkness, the bright Miami Beach light held at bay by Venetian blinds. When I turned on the lamp by the bed, two large pieces of framed art appeared on the bedroom wall, just above the chest of drawers. One depicted an ocean and a boat, and the other showed a scene of a cottage surrounded by a flower garden.

The light from the lamp shone onto a large book with gold edges and corners. The raised gold letters on the cover read, "Live Each Day to the Fullest." The book appeared to be a form of calendar, or a book of quotations. Slowly, I lifted the cover and saw "Love, Mother" written in flourishing longhand letters on the flyleaf. Feeling guilty about invading this nice man's privacy, I immediately let the cover fall back into place. As I looked more carefully at the room, I was excited to see a bookcase completely filled with what looked like impressive books. A large stuffed chair sat near the windows with a footstool in front of it, and I could just imagine my new friend reading in that chair, with his feet up. I couldn't help thinking of Mr. Hagan, and how happy he would have been to see all

113

those shining books.

Turning in the bed, I felt the luscious silk of my rescuer's tan pajamas, which he had thoughtfully left folded to the right of the bathroom door the night before. Even though I hadn't remembered Jerry saying the pajamas were for my use, I realized he must have meant for me to wear them, and I had delighted in slipping into them gingerly, instead of wearing the soiled cotton gown in my suitcase.

At first, the events that had brought me to this house seemed like a fairy tale. I thought I must be living in the Tale of the Three Bears, and I'd found just the right size bed, only I had been generously invited to enjoy it. I had a feeling that a magical transition for my entire life was in the process of happening. As I lay in the cozy bed, I needed some time to sort through my memories of the night before, because I couldn't quite tell what was real from what might have been just a dream. I turned my sore, stiff body over, and closed my eyes again, reluctant to awaken fully.

The only element of the dream I knew to be wholly real was Jerry Brady, the man who had almost run me over in his Cadillac. Yes, I knew he was real, because he had talked with me for several hours on his porch, before we had moved inside. Coming more to my senses and opening my eyes again to gaze at the books, the art, and the soft chair by the windows, I reassured myself that what I was seeing was not a dream based on the newspapered walls of my childhood, which had been covered with pictures of castles and famous people. It was Jerry's villa, as substantial and genuine as he was.

As we had continued our get-acquainted visit on his porch, I kept noticing the most affectionate expression on Jerry's face. His concern about my injuries had reminded me of Mr. Hagan's concern for my welfare on the day when he worried that he might have caused the neighbors to gossip about us. Although with Jerry I had at first been in a state of stunned wariness, gradually I started to look into his gentle eyes, and to understand that he was appealing to me to let him help, showing he sincerely felt responsible for my injuries. The ocean waves, only a few hundred yards away, had started to orchestrate a mighty crescendo of hope, whereas just an hour earlier, those waves had been laden with the gloom of a funeral dirge.

Jerry had pleaded, "Miss Warren, please let us go to a hospital, where the doctor can examine you and see if you might have serious wounds. That was a fierce tumble on the cement."

"No, I'm really okay," I said, feeling embarrassed about my unkempt appearance and my need for a full bath. I hadn't even thought of how untended my body had been, when I had been sitting in the sand at dusk the evening before, rehearsing my plans for my own drowning. Now my sense of physical untidiness seemed magnified as I sat on Jerry's clean porch, sinking into the softness of that fancy white couch.

"Please," Jerry said, "because you're limping, you may need medical attention. If you won't agree to see a doctor, would you be more comfortable letting me help you get home? Perhaps there you would be among your family, and we could decide what action might be most appropriate. You must understand that I feel responsible, and please know how much I have worried. Now that I have miraculously been privileged to meet you, I want to make amends."

"Why? It wasn't your fault. I shouldn't have been jaywalking."

He smiled, showing beautiful, healthy teeth. "I must tell you," he said, "I totally abhor the word 'should.' I feel it would be a great service to humanity if it were taken out of the dictionary."

I thought that comment sounded like something Mr. Hagan might have said, or Ralph Waldo Emerson himself. And of course, his mention of the word "dictionary" brought Mr. Hagan vividly to mind, but again I let the thought of my cherished mentor slide right back out, because I had to hold fast to what was happening in this astonishing present moment.

I decided then to tell Jerry about my situation, starting with my Grandma's death. I described what had happened at the boarding house, and how I had found myself homeless. As I spilled out my story, I expected Jerry to feel sympathy, for I had already sensed he was a compassionate man, but I was startled when he was so moved that his eyes brimmed with tears. One tear dropped onto his trousers, making a wet spot the size of a quarter.

With his hand he rubbed his eyes as he said, "Miss Warren, may I call you Dean?"

"Of course, please do."

"As I see it, we have got to get you out of this unfortunate situation."

"I'd be most grateful, and when I get my next check from where I work . . ."

As Jerry waved his hand in front of his face, as if to say *Don't worry about your next check,* I could not help noticing how well-manicured his hands were. I was reminded of Mr. Leach's fancy hands when he had reached down one summer day in Georgia to help me pluck the feathers off a fryer Mommy and I were dressing for his family. As a child of parents whose rough hands showed their constant hard work, I had been so impressed by Mr. Leach's soft, clean hands. They had seemed to represent a luxurious way of life.

Just then I realized that the bracing, lemony fragrance I noticed in Jerry's presence was the same as the aroma I had always enjoyed around Mr. Leach! As a child, I had thought it was simply the smell of rich people. Now I realized Jerry and Mr. Leach must have used the same cologne or aftershave lotion.

Jerry stood up and said, "Dean, let's not worry about the details just now. You cannot be sleeping on the streets. I can help."

As he extended his hand toward me, and helped me up, he added, "Let's go inside and figure out what to do."

Coming into his home, I felt as if I was entering a picture in a

magazine, filled with cream-colored furniture, art, and flowers.
Jerry held my hand again as he helped me sit slowly down on a couch. I hadn't needed assistance during the previous couple of days, when I had managed to ignore the pain of my injured legs, but now I felt myself contentedly yielding to his concerned attention.
Jerry then pulled forward a straight-backed chair with a needlepoint seat cover – much more graceful than the cane-bottomed chairs of my childhood – and sat down, with his knees almost touching mine.
A candlelight bulb cast a rosy glow on everything. With an intoxicating sense, as thrilling as my first joyous glimpses into the life of a writer as I read Emerson on Mr. Hagan's porch, I imagined that rosy glow might be coming from my own eyes instead of from the light bulb.

Jerry sat for an entire minute in silence, with his hands clasped and his fingers touching his chin, as if in a prayer mode, and I began to wonder if I should be afraid of this man who appeared to be so good. This was not a situation that had ever been addressed during my upbringing – what to expect when someone had rescued you and brought you into his home, under the guise of friendliness. Quickly though, a more logical idea struck me. I doubted that this well-dressed man, with a fragrance of cologne, would be attracted to a young woman who looked and smelled as I did, having not had a bath for so many days, I had barely had a chance to clean my wounds thoroughly, or to cover them with bandages. Kindness to people in need was something with which I was familiar, since my family and neighbors had always generously shared what little they had with those who needed help.

At long last, Jerry lifted his head, looking benevolently at me. "Here's what I think we could do," he said. "Let me know what you think about my plan. I have a brother living near here in Coral Gables, and I need to visit him and his wife, who have just returned after having been attached to the Italian Embassy this past year. I could telephone him and say I have a friend who needs to spend some days here in Miami Beach, and that I'd like to stay with them."

Jerry was already getting up from his chair and moving it back to its original place against the wall, filled with energy about this solution. "Is that alright with you, Dean, to stay here in my villa for a few days as you recuperate? You would be safe here. And I could come by to make sure you're getting better."

Speechless as I was, I managed to say, "If you are sure, I would certainly appreciate it."

Heading toward the door to his bedroom, Jerry turned back to say, "My brother is a retired Army General, Francis M. Brady, and his wife hails from Texas. She's an heiress to the Texaco oil company."

My mind went into a tizzy -- a General! I had come from generations of military hero worshippers. My family had always been grateful to the soldiers who had fought gallantly to save our little farm and those of our neighbors near Ellijay.

119

From the bedroom, as Jerry started to dial the phone, he told me a little more about his brother's accomplishments and I felt sure his string of chatter was meant to make me feel comfortable. The memory of that conversation has given me many chuckles through the years. He almost sounded as if he was trying to impress me.

Now I heard Jerry on the phone. "Hello...oh fine, and how are you and Anne? Great! I just wanted to mention, I have a friend who needs a place to stay for a few days. Would you and Anne put me up? I would love a visit with you." He appeared to be listening to his brother's response, and then he said, "Fine. Thanks. I'll be over in an hour or so."

Jerry came back into the living room to sit beside me on the sofa, but quickly jumped up again.

"Oh, I just realized, we need to get your things from your boarding house."

Half an hour later, with the aid of Jerry's flashlight, we had collected my clothes and personal items. I wasn't sure where I would be sleeping after the next few nights, but for now I was relieved to be safe.

Once we were back inside Jerry's house, he busied himself telling me all the facts he thought I needed to know about the dishwasher, the clothes washer and dryer, the lights, and the Venetian blinds. I walked close beside him among his lovely rooms and his sparkling kitchen. As soon as he showed me his bathroom, I exclaimed, "This is where I can't wait to spend a couple of hours!"

"Alright," Jerry said, smiling. "I'll be off then. I hope you enjoy your whole stay here."

He placed a slip of paper on a small living room table.

"Please call me here at my brother's house if you need me. And if you could follow me to the door, I'll show you the inside lock."

As Jerry handed me the key at the front door, he added, with a hopeful look on his face, "If it's alright with you, I'll come pick you up for breakfast at Pumperniks tomorrow morning. I'll only be a half hour away, and I think you and I could use a good breakfast."

I couldn't help starting to cry, out of a mixture of gratitude and fatigue. "How can I ever repay you for all you are doing for me?" I said through my tears.

He reached to give my shoulder a soft pat. "My pay is in finding you safe after the near collision with my car!"

I wiped my eyes and smiled.

"Please say a big thank you for me to your white Cadillac," I said, and then I watched him disappear in the darkness.

Some hours later, after a soothing bath, I jumped into bed, totally exhausted but blissfully happy.

As I stretched out in the big bed now, I realized that this day held the promise of being much better than a dream. In less than an hour Jerry Brady would be back here, as promised, to take me to Pumperniks for a hearty Sunday breakfast. I would worry later

121

about what would happen next. I just wanted to enjoy a brief respite from my troubles. I couldn't believe I would soon be with him, inside that popular deli restaurant I'd walked past so often.

I stared at Johnny's old suitcase, which I had never totally unpacked after my airplane trip. Reaching into the suitcase, I brought out my best navy skirt. It had large wrinkles in it, since I hadn't had any electricity to iron it at the boarding house. My white blouse was even more creased and in need of smoothing with an iron, but since I didn't have time to iron it, and the weather was cool, I draped my soft blue sweater around my shoulders to hide some of the ridges in the blouse. Then I opened the blinds to let in the sunlight.

The doorbell rang and I nervously rushed to open it. There stood Jerry smiling, wearing a cream-colored, stylish Izod short-sleeved sport shirt, tan trousers and brown loafers, his hair neatly groomed. He looked like a character in the movies, perhaps like one played by Cary Grant, but personally, I already saw him only as the look alike of Queen Elizabeth's husband.

"Did you have a good night?" His first words rang like cheerful music to my ears on this heavenly bright morning of a new day.

During the walk with Jerry, I was filled with giddy joy. Most likely my giddiness sprang partly from relief. I had food and shelter and friendship, after so much worry. Even if this relief was temporary, it was real, and so welcome. I had had to carry a heavy burden for two years in Miami Beach, trying to manage a day job and a bar job. Yet now, walking with Jerry, I knew how supremely happy Cinderella must have felt as she danced at the ball.

As we neared the entrance to Pumperniks, the luscious smell of pastries baking grabbed my attention. It was the same tantalizing aroma that had caused me so recently to yearn to go inside and beg for a leftover piece from the customers' plates. Today would be different. I was going to eat a fresh pastry, straight from the oven.

A distinguished looking man with menus greeted Jerry energetically. I assumed he was the owner, since I had often seen him standing outside the door as I had walked past. On those days, he had appeared to be getting breaths of fresh air. I thought how glad I was that I had not used this restaurant's restroom. I would have been labeled a "vagrant" here, just as at Publix Market.

"Oh, Mr. Brady, it is so good to see you," the gentleman said. "We're all sorry when the racing season ends and you leave for the summer. Welcome back!"

Jerry reached for his hand and their firm, long clasp expressed much fondness between them.

"I'm always happy to see you also, Jeff. I miss talking with you and I also get hungry for your good food."

"Yes, Jerry, your friend Toots Shor's spot in New York may be an exciting place, but we have the best food, don't we?" He teased Jerry good-naturedly as he led us to a booth. "Your favorite booth, waiting for you."

Jerry said, "Oh, Jeff, I almost forgot. This is my friend Dean from Georgia."

"Pleased to meet you, Dean," Jeff said, bowing.

A number of people had called out friendly hellos as we passed their tables. Jerry seemed to know everyone here. Sitting side by side in a dark green booth, we looked at the menu. Each item looked more scrumptious than the one before. Soon the waiter came to take our orders, and Jerry turned to me.

"What would you like, Dean?"

Looking at the waiter, I spoke up happily.

"I would like bacon, two eggs over medium, an apricot Danish pastry and a cup of coffee."

Out of habit, I had ordered my favorite breakfast, which I'd always ordered for dinner at the bar, before I had to start work.

When the waiter left, Jerry leaned toward me and said, "Tell me about you and Georgia." I felt his attention was totally consumed with interest about me. Later I would learn that that would always be the way he made me feel in our conversations.

After a couple of delightful hours over breakfast, Jerry patted my hand as it rested on the table beside my empty plate and said, "Dear Dean, perhaps I should take you to my place now, so that you can get a full day of rest. I will be going to my office at the Tropical Park race track for the afternoon."

"Yes, thank you so much for the lovely breakfast."

As we started to walk out of the restaurant, Jerry gently

cupped my elbow with his hand. Although at first I soared, sensing a romantic connection, in the next moment I realized that he was more likely thinking I needed support in using my legs. We walked side by side through the large and brightly lit room of tables, with many warm greetings extended to "Jerry" or "Mr. Brady." One young man rose from his chair to shake Jerry's hand, and said, "I'll see you later at the track."

As Jerry and I slowly walked the two blocks to his villa, he told me he was the General Manager of American Totalisator, a company that rented their betting machines to all the thoroughbred racing tracks in the United States. During the winter season of racing, he went first to the Tropical Park in Miami, then to the track at Hialeah, Florida. He attended early spring racing at the Gulfstream Track, and in May, he returned to his home in The Delmonico Hotel in New York City for the summer racing season in the northeast. Hearing Jerry's schedule for the first time, I thought his life sounded colorful and glamorous, although I couldn't comprehend living in that way, with more than one home. If the thought had occurred to me that I would ever live in two places, and travel to Florida each winter, I would have shrugged it off as just another of my wild dreams.

While Jerry was exchanging greetings with various friends along the way, I walked a few paces ahead. Glimpsing myself in the windows outside Pumperniks as we left, I was struck again by how messy I looked, from the shoddy run-down heels of my shoes to the top of my untidy hair. At least my hair was clean, since my shower the night before, yet it looked in need of a good haircut, just as I looked in need of new clothes. I worried that everyone but Jerry must have been critical of my appearance. He, however, seemed happily oblivious.

Once Jerry caught up with me, I relaxed, as I basked in his affection. He told me that I'd won quite a few compliments from his friends, who asked him where he'd found such a pretty young woman. For the first time in my life, I felt like one of the beautiful people who were in the newspapers on the walls of my family home. I decided to enjoy the moment.

9: Lincoln Road Shopping

Five days later, when Jerry dropped me off at his house after dinner, he suggested that the next morning -- a Saturday -- would be perfect for shopping. I had been going to work each morning, and having dinner with Jerry each night.

"I have a feeling you'd enjoy having some new clothes," he said simply.

"I would! but . . ."

How could I tell Jerry my doubts? What would Mommy and Daddy think of him buying me clothes? What should I think of it?

Jerry seemed to read my mind, because he just waved his hand in the air, as if to say, *Don't worry about a thing! It's just a little something! No strings attached!*

"I would be so happy and honored to help you in this one small way, Dean. You deserve to have clothes that make you feel special, because you *are* a very special person."

I thanked him, and he said, "That's settled, then. How about if we go to my friend Joan's shop?"

He opened a magazine to show me pictures of her place. Instantly, I could see how swanky and high fashion it was. Reading the captions under the photos of the glamorous models, I read that her store was called a "dress salon." "Salon" was a new word for me, and I wasn't sure if the accent should be on the "a" as in "saylon." Since my little dictionary was packed in my suitcase inside one of Jerry's closets, I hoped to wait on saying that word until I heard someone else pronounce it.

On Saturday morning, I awakened early, knowing I needed to work at putting together a suitable outfit and a decent pair of shoes so that I could be ready for our shopping date. As soon as the doorbell rang, I rushed to open the door. With my heart pounding, I took in the vision of Jerry's smiling face, as he stood on the front porch holding bags of groceries. A rush of joy flooded my being as Jerry walked in, and I breathed deep, taking in that "rich people" fragrance. I walked beside him to the kitchen, where he unloaded the fresh fruit, milk, cheese, orange juice and vegetables into the refrigerator, and placed a freshly baked loaf of bread in the bread box.

Since it seemed words of gratitude were inadequate, I wished I could rush and hug him, yet I dared not, since his attitude suggested precise and correct behavior, even though he was most warmly spontaneous and attentive to me. I wondered if he would ever think of me romantically.

"How was your night, dear Dean?" he asked, as he opened a new tin of coffee and started to fill the coffee pot with water.

"It couldn't have been better."

"Oh, but tonight I think is going to be better."

Jerry's clear, sparkling hazel eyes were twinkling like those of a young child offering his mother a surprise.

I tried in that instant, as I often did, to focus on Jerry as a fallible human being, even though I had not seen a fault. Otherwise, I thought I might melt. Each moment near him I was becoming more filled with tenderness in the wonder of his rapt attention. True, I knew logically that I had better make an effort to stop imagining Jerry as some magical fairy tale prince who had the power to whisk me away to Never Never Land. A hard shell of self-protectiveness kept reminding me that Jerry was simply a man, and might disappoint me. The experiences I had endured in the bar had left me thoroughly convinced that I never wanted a man to touch me ever again. Only a few days earlier, I had been eager to sink into the ocean waves and experience the mysteries of eternity, out of reach of any male's aggressive hands. I had felt sure that would be heaven. Yet Jerry was different. He had proven himself to be consistently respectful with me, and he had made no lusty moves, much as I was beginning to wish he would.

Once the coffee had brewed, I reached into the cabinet for cups and saucers. I had already had a hearty breakfast.

"Come, let's sit," Jerry said, as he sat down at the dining table and patted the seat of the chair beside him. I slid onto the chair's needlepoint cushion.

"I have news I wish to share with you." He smiled as he handed me a key on a gold chain. "This is the key to your new apartment. My friend Fred has made it available for you. It's yours free for the entire year. So you will not need to move again for some time."

I gazed at that key in the palm of my hand. It seemed the words he had spoken were not registering in my mind, yet I understood that the key represented freedom and security. Stunned, I let it drop to the floor. Jerry bent to retrieve it.

"I cannot possibly accept such a gift," I said, trembling as he placed the key back into my hand and cupped it in a loving way.

Jerry shrugged and smiled, as he explained, "It's an apartment Fred wasn't able to rent for this winter season, so it's not as if he's losing any money on it."

By now I was familiar with his graceful way of making me feel that all the things he was doing for me were no bother at all -- sweetly assuring me that no one was being inconvenienced in the least. Still, I felt uncertain about receiving such a big and important gift from him -- my own apartment, for a whole year.

We finished our coffee as I tried to hide any clue that I was still in a daze of unbelief and doubt. Jerry stood up and beckoned to me.

"Come, let's go see the apartment. I'm familiar with it, since Fred has had it available before, for some of my out-of-town business clients. Much as I love having you here in my place, I think my landlord is getting suspicious that I have kidnapped a beautiful young lady, plus the fact that my brother and his wife may have had about enough of me waking them up each night when I come in." He laughed. "Actually, Fran asked me last evening if I had forgotten that we boys had a curfew. So in keeping with my stellar reputation of being a good guy who honors family traditions, I must return home."

As I listened to Jerry talk about his upbringing, I became a bit calmer. I was beginning to learn to trust Jerry's giving heart. The following years would bring more and more evidence of his natural generosity. He had a special, quiet way of making me feel comfortable and emphasizing how important it was for him to make me happy. I started to realize too that Jerry liked me so much that my own happiness gave him pleasure.

Now Jerry looked at the clock beside his kitchen window. "Dear Dean," he said, "we have chatted so long, I see we are running very late with our date to meet Joan at her shop. Let's wait until tomorrow morning to see your new apartment, because right now I have a really nice restaurant in Coconut Grove that I would love for us to go to this evening. It's on the other side of Miami. Shall we go find you a beautiful dress?"

My shopping date with Jerry still shines as brightly in my memory as the Miami sun. It was a day I shall always cherish, because it was the first time in my life when I had gone into a store without a fixed amount that I could spend. All my years previously, I would shop with a worry in the back of my mind that my check might bounce.

Feeling as if a magic wand had suddenly turned me into a princess, I sat beside Jerry in that comfortable white Cadillac as we glided smoothly down Collins Avenue. The gold-crested row of hotels shone in all their glory, a sight I had often missed that year, as I sat in the bus with tired eyes closed on my way home from work, though with a sense of gratitude that I did have a job and a room at the boarding house.

Turning right onto Lincoln Road, we immediately entered the parking lot of Joan Gaines Fashions, and Jerry parked the car. Ever the gentleman, he held my elbow as we walked inside. Perhaps seeing that I was a bit nervous, he pointed to the large, exquisitely carved mahogany door and started a bit of casual conversation.

"That dark sedate door looks a bit out of place here amid the gaudy glamour of Miami Beach, doesn't it, Dean? But I think it's in keeping with Joan's New York background. I've often thought she must have felt she needed to bring a little of her past here. She's a former star of the Ziegfeld Follies Dancers. She's married to a close friend of mine, Ben Gaines."

I'm sure he meant his words to make me feel more at ease. Instead, this description of Joan Gaines' life jolted me into remembering the wide difference between Jerry's and my worlds.

He was a sophisticated New Yorker and I was clearly a grubbing-to-survive country girl from the mountains.

As Jerry held the door for me, I stepped inside, sinking into a couple of inches of soft, thick beige carpet. It was then that my bubble really burst. I thought of how frumpy my worn and faded clothes must look. The soles of my scuffed heels had already sunk out of sight, and I wished the rest of my shaggy self could vanish too.

A slender, petite lady rushed to welcome us. With her short hair style and youthful skin, she looked as if she had stopped aging when the Vaudeville era had ended, over twenty years earlier. She ran to give Jerry a huge hug. As his strong arms lifted her, she looked down from above his shoulder and discovered me, standing there feeling shy and uncomfortable. Her face fell as she touched the floor.

Extending his arm toward me, Jerry said, "Joan, this is my lovely friend, Dean Warren."

"Nice to meet you, Miss Warren," she coolly said, and in the next breath added, "I'm being signaled back to the designing room."

She waved to a clerk to come and take care of me, her body language indicating that she was through with me. Jerry cupped my elbow again and winked at me protectively, as a stylishly dressed clerk with a half-smile appearing and disappearing under her rather long, aristocratic nose, tilted upward, escorted us into a large room with red velvet drapes covering a wall of windows. The soft light coming from ornate fixtures hanging from the ceiling cast a warm glow on all the ladies sitting along the runway. As we neared our chairs, I could glimpse the models standing behind the curtains, poised to enter.

Once Jerry was sitting close beside me under the flattering lights, I felt a little more at ease. Several fancily dressed ladies seated along both sides of the runway waved at Jerry, while some of the ones standing nearby smiled and spoke to him as if he were a close friend. Soon all the ladies and a few men sat down and the show started. One of the models blew a kiss at Jerry as she stepped upon the platform of the runway. The wealthy customers exchanged soft remarks about the dresses the models were wearing. While most of the people carefully scrutinized the models, I noticed that several of the women seemed unable to keep from glancing at me and just as quickly casting their eyes away. I realized that, in spite of my modest clothes, I was much younger than these women, and clearly I had a well-liked admirer at my side.

After asking my opinion about certain styles, and ordering a few dresses for me, Jerry told me that he wanted to talk to Joan for a minute.

He gave me his familiar, comforting pats on my shoulder and waved as he headed back to the designing room.

Soon a lovely middle-aged saleswoman who introduced herself as Kate led me into a dressing and fitting room, where a rack of dresses and matching shoes had been rolled in. I fit into the dresses perfectly and Kate complimented me on my slim model's body. My thought flew back to my Grandma, Mommy and Aunt Ibby. When they had made dresses for me years earlier, they often said I was so skinny that the boys would think I was not healthy enough to raise a family. That memory brought a smile as I thought perhaps in these different surroundings my skinny body was going to work well for me.

I heard a door close in a room on the other side of the fitting room wall. Then I heard Jerry's voice.

"Dean is one of the most endearing women I have met in many years." He paused a few seconds and then added, "Joan, I've never met anyone who touched me so deeply."

A long silence followed and I wished I could have looked through the wall and seen her face. Finally she spoke.

"Jerry, I speak to you as an older sister, and I assume you surely know how Ben and I love you. Please tread carefully. She is just a child."

Jerry answered as if he had missed the implication of what she was trying to impart to him. I understood her implication, however, and felt a shock at this first glimpse of some people's perception of our relationship. I looked much too young for him, I gathered, even though I was actually in my late twenties, and had had some experience in the world.

"Yes, Joan," Jerry said, and his voice mounted to an excited pitch. "Your remark relates to something I wanted to mention earlier.

Would you choose some styles for Dean that could make her look more mature, to match me?"

Another silence followed. Then Joan's voice came coldly, with a matter-of-fact tone.

"Jerry, my designing career is built on making matrons look like teenagers, not making teenagers look like matrons."

The closing of the door ended my eavesdropping. I was very confused. Even Jerry was feeling a difference in our ages that I couldn't see. I knew he was older, but I could only think of his age as part of his attractiveness.

Soon the clerk led me to Joan's office near the front of the store, where Jerry was waiting for me. She had a notebook with a list of styles that she felt were good for me, along with Jerry's suggestions from the runway. A young uniformed man slowly rolled a cart past us, filled with boxes of my new clothes.

Through the window I could see a dapper man with greying hair and a huge friendly smile emerging from a long black limousine. As Jerry and I walked through the foyer of the store, on our way out, this man rushed up to embrace Jerry. Then he focused on me, smiling warmly.

Jerry said, "Dean, this is my dear friend Ben, Joan's husband. Ben, my dear young friend, Dean."

Ben reached forward and hugged me heartily as he grasped my hand.

Again I felt I was in a movie scene, where all the actors and actresses were so polished and perfectly behaved. Ben's genial handshake and hug gave me the feeling that he genuinely liked me, and his open presence helped me forget the aloofness of the other people I had met in Joan's shop. It occurred to me that the people who had been most aloof had all been women. Jerry's male friends had welcomed me with enthusiasm.

After a few minutes of our conversation with Ben, Joan appeared at the door and called, "Jerry, a call from your office."

Jerry excused himself and followed Joan back inside to take the call.

Ben motioned for me to sit in a large beige chair as he moved a straight chair and took a seat in front of me. A huge diamond ring glittered from his finger. I thought that diamond seemed to contradict his down to earth nature. I had never seen a diamond on a man's finger before.

"So you're from Atlanta, I hear. Atlanta is one of my favorite cities, especially in the springtime, with the white dogwood blossoms, and early spring flowers everywhere."

He added that many people told him they liked autumn best in North Georgia, with the colorful trees on the majestic mountains. "But I still prefer Georgia springtimes."

I wondered if he knew how sweet his words were to me as he expounded on the hills and streams that had given me such joy in my childhood. I immediately felt a kinship, but I wasn't yet prepared to believe that charming Ben would become a great source of joy and strength for me through the coming years.

Just then, Jerry returned with the news that some problems had developed and he would need to get to his office at the race track right away.

"I must rush on also," said Ben, "since I'm already late for an appointment. When Joan telephoned me that you were here, I wanted to drop by and welcome Dean to our circle."

I felt my mouth stretch with a smile. I really needed to hear Ben's sincere welcome. He reached for my hand again and flashed me a smile.

As Ben turned to go, he suddenly turned back to me and said, "Miss Warren."

Jerry corrected him. "Dean."

"Dean, how would you like to join Joan and me, Jerry, and the Sullivans for a cruise to Nassau next weekend? We've been planning to take this trip for some time. Now that the Sullivans are here in Miami Beach, it would be a good time to take a vacation. We always love the island. Have you been there?"

Jerry turned to me. "Dean, would you like to come? I would love to have you with us. I'm sure your boss would be okay with you taking Thursday and Friday off, wouldn't he?"

"Yes, I'm sure he would," I said, though I was feeling a bit stunned at the swift planning of such a weekend. Although I clearly felt a powerful attraction to Jerry, and he had just bought me clothes,

I could not be completely sure how he felt about me. In all our evenings together that week, we hadn't even kissed. I wondered too what other people might think of my accepting expensive clothes and an invitation to a cruise. Yet, in the next instant, I let my anxious questions go. I decided to trust my instincts about Jerry's good intentions.

Once Jerry had dropped me off at his villa, I dreamed about my new wardrobe, safely tucked inside that white Cadillac until Jerry could return tomorrow morning for our habit of having Sunday breakfast at Pumperniks. After that, Jerry's plan was to move my things to my new apartment by about noon.

It was a quiet late afternoon. I prepared myself a fancy lunch of artichoke hearts and roasted peppers from Jerry's bountiful supply. Again I had a chance to telephone Mr. Jones in Ellijay. Through him, I sent a message to my parents and told them to call me "at my girlfriend's home." Tomorrow, I realized, it would be good to be living in my own apartment, where I would have my own telephone. I would be happy to stop lying to Mommy and Daddy about where I was living.

That night I snuggled into the delicious smelling bed. Instead of counting sheep as I had done in earlier years, I began to count all those lovely clothes parading by on the fashion models. The best part was the realization that so many of those dresses and shoes were now definitely mine.

139

Cozy in this house of Jerry's, I also counted my blessings. I felt amazed that our relationship had moved so quickly. Our paths had crossed only a week earlier, and I had gone from contemplating suicide to feeling happy and secure. I fell asleep wrapped in the joy of knowing that Jerry cared deeply about my well-being. Other people observing us, like Joan Gaines, might have felt cynical about a young woman with a wealthy older man, but I simply felt lucky.

As it happened, it would be another three months before I had my chance to be on the yacht with Jerry, but it would be well worth the wait.

Figure 2: Modeling for Joe Levy's Frocks in Miami

Figure 3: Jerry, my prince, just before I met him

10: The Bar Girl Models

The following morning, a bright and early Sunday, I collected all I owned, in preparation for the move to my new home: a couple of shopping bags containing my toiletries and a few odds and ends, Johnny's shabby suitcase filled with second-hand clothes and the dictionary Mr. Hagan had given me.

Already it was 8 a.m. My mind was extra busy, thinking that in a matter of hours I would see my new apartment for the first time and spend the afternoon unpacking those clothes Jerry had bought for me, which would soon be placed inside my very own closet.

I was so eager to see inside those boxes that I would have preferred to skip my breakfast. As soon as I realized this, I paused. Was I the same young woman who one week earlier had not had any food at all and had stopped short of going behind a restaurant to see if I might scrounge a piece of coffee cake or bacon from the garbage?

As I placed Johnny's worn suitcase beside the front door, my heart filled with strong emotions. I felt I needed to move Jerry's needlepoint-bottomed chair beside the suitcase so that I could sit in silence, to recall the day Johnny had gone to Michigan. A week before, he had bought only twelve Budweisers instead of his usual twenty-four, so that he could buy a newer suitcase at the pawn shop and give me his old one, with the expectation that I would follow him soon. I could still picture as clear as day Johnny's face as we stood next to his brother's car and said goodbye. In my second year in Miami, Johnny had filed for divorce, and I had gladly signed the papers, relieved to be freed at last. A month or two after that, I discovered through my parents that Johnny had married a woman in Michigan and was very happy.

Surrounded by the luxury of Jerry's villa, and aware of Jerry's warm generosity toward me, I could think of Johnny with sympathy. I realized with new clarity that I should forgive Johnny for what I had perceived to be his messing up of my life. In like manner, I felt the need to forgive myself for my own part in our unfortunate marriage, including my decision to move far away without his knowledge.

In that instant, I felt lighter in spirit. I experienced a total release from our miserable entanglement and ready to move on with new confidence and a clear heart. The Universe had graced me with a divine nudge to forgive Johnny and myself, and with this forgiveness came a sense of freedom incomparable to anything I had ever felt. I hoped his life could be as happy as mine. I was sure that he must be better off without me. This pause to assess, forgive and put closure on our relationship boosted my sense of contentedness and hopefulness on this special morning.

When the doorbell rang, I quickly collected myself and moved the chair back to its spot by a table, that was topped by a vase of daisies. I gave a heartfelt smile to Jerry as I opened the door.

"Good morning, my little Dean," he said, and soon we were off to breakfast.

As we walked into Pumperniks, we enjoyed the usual flurries of good morning greetings and "Happy-to-see-you-again-this-winter-season" comments among Jerry and his friends. Soon we were seated in Jerry's favorite booth. While we waited to be served, I told Jerry how I had been coming to terms with both Johnny's and my mistakes, forgiving both of us. I assured him how ready I felt for a new life, and how happy I was to be with him. He listened intently and then changed his position in our corner booth so that we could look into each other's eyes.

"Dean," he said earnestly, "thank you so much for your openness. I am very touched by all that you're saying. This is an important time for both of us, because it opens up our relationship to something more. I am hopeful now that you and I may have a chance to come to know each other better."

He touched the back of my hand, and as his hand lingered, I placed my other hand warmly on his.

Jerry became slightly awkward and shy, as he opened up to me more fully than he ever had before.

"Some years ago," he said in a quiet voice, "I had somewhat the same experience of the need to forgive and forget past hurts. I was once married to a beautiful dancer, who, with her partner, was quite celebrated internationally. Upon my return home to New York from the racing season in Florida, some years ago, I was met with disappointment. She had fallen in love with a photographer for *Look* magazine and wanted a divorce so she could marry him."

Our conversation that morning turned out to offer a chance for Jerry's real character to shine through. I started to feel more confident that he genuinely wanted to help me and that he placed no price tag on his generosity. I now knew that my angel Prince was giving me the chance of which I had always dreamed..

We were soon on our way to my new apartment -- beautiful, modern and only a few blocks from Jerry's villa. For the first time in my life, I would have a room of my own. More than a room, in fact: a large immaculate living room, plus a bedroom, kitchen, and dining room, in addition to a spacious terrace extending from the back door to a secluded flower garden. A dense hedge of palm trees and banana trees made a thick green wall encircling the back fence. The only thing I could have wished for was a clothes line! But, alas, no clothes line in this fancy area of Miami Beach!

As soon as Jerry had placed all the boxes of clothes in the living room, he glanced at his watch and said, "I'm so sorry, but I must be going, dear Dean, since I'm already late for an appointment."

As he turned toward the door, he gave me two warm pats on my shoulder, and this time blew a kiss into my hair as he bent down to my head before reaching for the door.

"I'd love to take you by my friend Lou Walters' Copacabana nightclub tonight. Would you like that? Lou is the father of Barbara Walters, who's been making news lately."

He looked at me for signs of excitement and recognition, and I refrained from telling him I didn't know who he was talking about.

"You may have read about her in *The Miami Herald*," he added hopefully. "She's becoming quite successful internationally in her career in television journalism."

"Of course, I'd love that!"

Poking his head back inside the door, he said, "Oh, and I was just wondering -- would you please wear that little black dress with the string of pearls? I would so love to see you in it once again, before you start dressing in all those fancier clothes."

I was surprised for a moment, but I said, "I'll do that," as he closed the door behind him.

I pondered his wish as I opened the boxes of new clothes, pressing my nose into each dress and blouse to smell that scent of "rich people."

Amidst my unpacking that afternoon, I floated through my new apartment, inspecting the pretty furniture and the plush chairs, and marveling at the spaciousness of all the rooms. Deep rushes of gratitude swept me along as I touched the toaster, the stove, the fridge, the windows, the shelves, the coffee table, the flowers, and the thick white bedspread and soft pillow on my high bed. It was my first time to see such an apartment, with the same rich feel as Jerry's villa. Only in magazine pictures, and in Jerry's house, had I seen such a grand way of living. I simply could not refrain from frequently interrupting my folding of clothes and hanging up of dresses to take another run through the rooms, then outside to the back terrace, where I gazed up at the bright blue sky and breathed a thankful prayer as I whispered over and over again, "All this is mine."

Suddenly, I felt I must send a message to my parents by way of the Cartecay Country store. I dialed the number and Mr. Jones quickly answered.

"Cartecay Grocery."

"Good afternoon, Mr. Jones. This is Odean Warren, calling from Miami Beach. Would you please get a message to my Daddy and Mommy that I have good news for them? And please tell them to call me as soon as they can."

"Odean, you sound mighty happy."

"I am!" I yelled into the phone. "My modeling job is now paying me a great deal more, and I am so happy I want to tell this to my Mommy and Daddy as soon as I can."

As usual, I felt a little guilty about lying to my parents. I was just so happy, however, that today the guilt was minimal. I knew my parents would be glad once they knew Jerry, but I couldn't bear the pain of seeing and feeling their disappointment should my relationship with Jerry disintegrate. Since, in the depth of my heart, I wasn't yet sure how strong our bond was, I certainly was not in a

148

position to convince my parents.

"Odean, I will surely get this message to them as soon as I can. I am so happy to hear your good news. Usually the news I need to pass on is that somebody's died or some bad news like that. Well, Odean, you were always a cheerful, hardworking girl, and now you sound like you have something to be really happy about, and I am glad for you."

It was perhaps the first time I had ever been grateful to send a message to my parents through Mr. Jones instead of speaking directly to them, because if they had heard my over-the-top voice, they would have felt my mental state was something to worry about.

After the phone call, I paused a moment and examined that beautiful beige modern telephone on my kitchen wall. It was such a joy to have my own private telephone. My Mommy and Daddy would be able to call me directly, whenever they could gain access to a phone.

Soon, however, I realized I had better concentrate on getting myself dressed for my nightclub date with Jerry. The afternoon had flown by, and he would be coming to pick me up in a little over an hour. Suddenly I heard myself speaking loudly to Grandma, as if she were right next to me in my big modern kitchen.

"Grandma, I wish you were here to enjoy all this with me and I could hug you. Though I realize you might scold and say, *Child, you are running around like a chicken with its head cut off.*"

I started to cry with relief, feeling how happy Grandma

would be for me now, since I was released from worry about how I could survive just one more day.

I breathed deeply, making an effort to control my emotions. It was time to enjoy a quick bath in that picture-perfect bathroom. I will always remember stepping into my own clean tub, filled with warm water, and luxuriating in the fragrance of good soaps and shampoo.

After my bath, I dressed in my old black dress, trying to ignore the longing to wear the new light blue satin dress with the double crinoline petticoat. The blue satin certainly seemed more appropriate, since we were going to a nightclub. I gave in to the impulse to slip on a fashionable pair of black patent leather pumps instead of my old shoes. Oh, those new shoes felt so good! I couldn't resist them, and felt pretty sure that Jerry would just smile when he saw them on my feet. I began sashaying around the room, catching glimpses of myself in the mirrors of my bedroom, frequently taking a peek again into my closet, to breathe in the scent of the dresses. On one side of my closet, I had hung the dresses for evenings out with Jerry, and on the other side, I had arranged a few tailored outfits, which would make me look like a successful office manager in the insurance company instead of the stenographer that I was.

Looking again at my feet in my new shoes, for the first time in my life I thought how nice my ankles looked. I realized I had never really noticed them before. I remembered how unattractive and rough they had looked in the old corn-hoeing field shoes I had worn as a girl in Georgia. Now my legs and ankles were a vision as graceful as Queen Elizabeth's, in the photograph I had seen of her as she stepped from the carriage with Prince Philip, just after their marriage.

Then into my thoughts came the scene of my childhood on that jelly-making day when Grandma and Mommy had pointed to the pictures of Princess Elizabeth and her sister Margaret on the newspapered wall beside the stove.

Grandma had said, "Them girls are princesses and they look just like you girls and are the same age as you are."

Mommy placed her sewing in her lap and smiled big. She seemed proud of the fact that she had two girls who looked like the Queen of England's daughters. It strikes me now that Queen Elizabeth and her Prince are the only ones still living in this story about my Grandma, Mommy, and Colleen. Of course, the Queen and her handsome husband don't know my little family secret of look-alikes.

As the sun was setting, Jerry arrived and found me dressed and excitedly bubbling to him about all the fun I had had that day exploring my new home and unpacking the clothes. Once inside Jerry's Cadillac, taking care that he didn't see me, I took a few seconds to touch the soft leather beige seat. For a fleeting moment, I remembered the screeching brakes, which had stopped this car from hitting me. As Jerry drove, from the corner of my eye I saw he was smiling indulgently, as he listened to my happy description of the afternoon.

Soon we approached the magnificent nightclub, the Latin Quarter. I had often read about this club in the *Miami Herald* and had seen so many pictures of celebrities entering and exiting, that the Art Deco front looked familiar, with its elegantly curved steps and "Latin Quarter" in neon lights above.

I saw a sign for "Valet Parking," but had no idea what it meant. I thought I would look that word "valet" up in Mr. Hagan's dictionary when I returned home. As Jerry stopped the car, immediately two uniformed young men greeted him.

"Mr. Brady," they chimed together, smiling broadly.

As one of the young men opened Jerry's door, the other one opened mine. Jerry then walked around the car to guide me toward the unusually wide gold door.

As we entered, the Maître d' (I learned his title later) rushed to greet us, saying, "Oh Mr. Brady, come this way. Mr. Walters is waiting for you."

He led us through the dark room to a table at ringside of the stage. From the first instant I met Lou Walters, I found him to be a charming man. He gallantly seated me between Jerry and himself.

After the initial introductions and pleasantries, Jerry said, "Lou, it's wonderful how well Barbara is doing in her news reporting."

"Yes, I am so proud of her," Lou said, reaching for a large book on the shelf behind him. "I'm keeping a scrapbook!"

"First, let's show Dean the album of Barbara's childhood pictures." Jerry looked at me and smiled. "Barbara has been a star in this club since she was a girl."

Those albums were my introduction to the now famous Barbara Walters. During the following years, I would sit at that same table and watch her proud father glow with each succeeding year that his library of her photographs grew, along with her national and international popularity.

Jerry said, "Lou, when Barbara next comes home, perhaps the four of us could have a date together."

"That would be great," Lou said.

"People would think we were both out with our daughters," Jerry said, grinning.

"Oh no, no, never would anyone think I am old enough to be Barbara's father!" said Lou. He mockingly shook his head with its thinning, gray-streaked hair.

As the evening progressed, the chairs around our table filled with friends and famous celebrities of that era. Comedian Sid Caesar joined us, and so did Milton Berle, whose face I had indeed seen in the car that evening when I first met Jerry. Sid Caesar, who could be so boisterous as a comedian, surprised me by being polite and reserved. In contrast, Milton was talkative and sarcastic. Although I later learned that many people felt he was putting them

153

down with his biting sense of humor, I never took offense. I just listened intently to him. He liked that and called me a "sponge." I decided to believe this was a compliment!

Soon a handsome and fashionably dressed man wearing a pink shirt caught my attention. As he approached our table, Jerry said, "Dean, this is my good friend, Joseph Levy. Joe, I would like you to meet my young friend, Dean Warren."

Joe graciously shook my hand. I felt comfortable with him right away. Like Jerry, he smiled a lot and many people seemed to know and like him. I discovered that Joe had a highly successful business manufacturing women's clothing.

After an hour or so of watching chorus girls dancing, I was convinced the announcer was speaking the truth when he said, "These are the world's most gorgeous dancers." I had no previous knowledge of dancing showgirls. I only knew they were so glamorous, they looked unreal.

After the show, Joe turned his attention to me and asked, "Dean, have you ever modeled?"

I blushed and laughed. "No!" I said. I wondered if Joe could know how often I had wished to model, especially in this last glorious but slightly intimidating week among well-dressed people and celebrities. I blushed again as I thought of how I had been lying to my Mommy and Daddy about "my modeling job in Miami."

Joe said to Jerry, "I'd like you to bring Dean by my place tomorrow and I'll introduce her to the manager of our Junior department. With that perky ponytail, and her wide-eyed innocent look, I think she'd fit in well." Lou turned to me. "How does that sound, Dean?"

I realized instantly that if I could land a modeling job, I would be able to stop lying to my parents. At first I felt too surprised and happy to respond.

With a trembling voice, I said, "What a wonderful opportunity for me. Thank you so much, Mr. Levy."

"Call me Joe! We're family here." He shook my hand. "Alright, young woman! See you tomorrow."

And so it proved that I would have a modeling job and a Miami Beach sense of family with Joe Levy and his wife Betty for many years to come.

As time went by, after that soaring day, I often felt the need to say to Jerry that I could not continue to accept his extreme generosity. His reply would be something lighthearted, to the effect that one day, when I was wealthy, he might allow me to repay him.

At other times he would declare teasingly, "I'm just getting on your good side, because *my* most wished-for dream now, after meeting you, is to forget the rat-race of my life and go to the farm and live with you and your family there! You could teach me many things about a peaceful life near the creek, listening to the birds singing. Really, Dean, I envy the joy and honesty you shared with your family."

Saying this, Jerry would close his eyes and cup his chin in his hands, as if he were thoroughly enjoying imagining my life. He never made any disrespectful remark about my heritage, such as the rough people in the bar had seemed to enjoy making. Even though they had just been teasing, it had hurt my heart, since I realized that the truly good and honest people in my precious family seemed not to be honored. One of the life skills I gained in that bar was the capacity to to listen patiently to ignorant comments about my childhood, like "It sounds like you come from poor white trash in the mountains of Georgia," and "Y'all is a Georgia cracker. Wish you had some of that moonshine liquor with you!"

During all the years that followed, Jerry possibly never realized the depth of my gratitude for the way he honored my family background. He always emphasized how wealthy he felt I had been, as a girl, in all the ways that mattered most, and he showed how glad he was to contribute his own material wealth to my family and me.

Usually Jerry would put a cap on our conversations about money with his familiar soft pat on my shoulder and a sincere comment like "You delight me no end, Dean, and I enjoy you thrilling over the new life I have been able to share with you."

As I came to know Jerry more deeply, I realized that his appreciation for my family's hard-working life connected to a larger belief in equality and justice. In fact, Jerry felt embarrassed by his

156

own brother Fran's opposite views. As I was to discover, it took all of Jerry's patience -- and a little geographical distance too -- to remain affectionate and forgiving with this sibling. Fran and Anne lived part of the year at their home in Coral Gables, Florida, and the rest of the year at their other home in Italy, where, after retiring from the Air Force, Fran had become attached to the American Embassy in Rome. Jerry did not fret about how little he saw his brother, because their philosophies of life were so different. He felt closer to his brother Bill, whom he often helped out financially.

Once Jerry spoke about his relationship with Fran in somewhat this manner:

"I care about Fran deeply and have the greatest respect for his stellar accomplishment in the Air Force during the Second World War. At the end of the war, however, he and Anne moved to Miami, where they became members of the Bath Club. Do you know what this club is?"

Jerry looked at me, his eyebrows raised. I shook my head.

"Well, Dean, the Bath Club is an exclusive club for what you might call blueblood Anglo-Saxon socialites." He sighed. "And Fran and Anne spend most of their time with friends in that club, when they're in Miami."

He became silent for a moment, then said, "I have never gone to a club where some of my friends would not be welcome."

It gave me pleasure to realize how similar Jerry's values were to those of my own family. He had not grown up rich, and his

157

acquired wealth had not clouded his belief in people's equality, and his effort to treat each person with respect. I couldn't wait for the day when my Mommy and Daddy could know what a good person he was.

Figure 4: Fontainebleau Hotel where I saw Frank Sinatra and the Rat Pack

11: Dinner with the Sullivans

The following Monday morning, I waited for Jerry to pick me up for work, as he had faithfully done each day the week before. For the first time, I had chosen to wear one of my new outfits to work: a smart navy suit, with a label saying "Coco Chanel of Paris." Although I had little idea who Coco Chanel was, I enjoyed the feel of this suit, especially the silk blouse. While the collar had a hint of lace, with white embroidered edges around the top, the blouse itself was not frilly, so I hoped it would be perfect both for the office and for meeting Jerry's closest friend, the famous entertainer Ed Sullivan.

Once I was in the car next to Jerry, I let myself have glimpses of his aristocratic profile against the rows of magnificent palm trees, as we slowly made our way down Collins Avenue amidst the height of the bustling tourist season.

At a traffic light, Jerry turned to smile at me.

"Dean, I'll pick you up at your office at about 5:30. Ed's agent has scheduled him and Sylvia to watch a singer named Roberta Sherwood perform later tonight, so they'll need to leave the restaurant about 8:30. Is that alright with you?"

"Of course."

I had noticed how Jerry was always making sure that

161

whatever he had planned was okay with me. I wondered if he would soon learn that I was so eager to be with him, at any time or place, that the ceremonious nicety of asking me my opinion was totally unnecessary.

Crossing the MacArthur Causeway with Jerry that bright winter morning, I thought of Tom, who had so kindly taken me to work in Miami each day for two whole years. I wished Tom could see me now -- all decked out in my new finery.

As we entered the insurance company parking lot, I pointed to the bench and said to Jerry, "A very kind man named Tom, who also lived in the boarding house, used to pick me up on that bench. Let's meet there."

"Yes, Dean, I've thought about the experience of you finding that particular boarding house and how you immediately made good friends. I don't think you're quite aware of it yet, but you have an irresistible quality that draws people to you."

I blushed and thanked him as he made his way around the car to open my door.

At the office, I was aware of the stir my outfit made, especially among the other women. During the morning, Hortense, the office manager, asked me if she could take me to lunch.

I proudly said, "Hortense, please let me take *you* to lunch."

Looking astonished, she said, "Let's go for lunch and we'll talk later about who pays."

I agreed, although because of my early training in independence from my parents, I strongly wished to treat her. I knew it would certainly give me happiness, especially since I had a very fat wallet. The evening before, Jerry had quietly stuffed large bills into my purse. I had said self-consciously, "I'll pay you back soon," but he had just waved my words off.

"Let's go by your bank tomorrow morning," he had said, "because I'd like to deposit funds in your account, enough for you to send some home. I would be so honored to do that."

At that moment, his secretary had called Jerry on my telephone, and our conversation about money had been postponed yet once more. I had to keep waiting for the opportunity to figure out how I was going to pay him back.

As I looked at the menu in the restaurant, Hortense complimented me on my appearance.
She quickly added, with a smile on her face, "These fabulous clothes you're wearing are causing quite a stir among the girls in the office, you know. We're all a bit jealous."

I was glad to see Hortense smile, since she was so serious in the office. Somehow, though, I realized I was in one of those "polite society" situations where it was necessary to search for hidden meanings in conversation. This was a new skill for me to learn, since in my childhood area of Appalachia people always spoke as they felt, and in that way you knew their full meaning.

When the waiter had taken our order and left the table, I felt I

163

should say something, but wasn't sure what it could be.

"You know, dear," Hortense said, "I'm not trying to be nosy, but I see a great and sudden change in you, and I'm concerned for you. I feel a bit like an aunt to you, you know, Dean. Though nothing could please me more than to see you happy with legitimate good fortune."

I gathered from her emphasis on the word "legitimate" that she was guessing I had gone back to the bar or had become a call-girl, in order to be able to afford such nice clothes. Her suggestion pained me, since each scene in my relationship with Jerry had shown him to be so kind and caring, with deep feeling for me. Looking at Hortense's "holier-than-thou" face, I felt that same disgust I had experienced when the preacher told my parents how our neighbors were talking about me behind my back. I remembered how the preacher had urged me not to spend so much time reading with Mr. Hagan, since our relationship could look questionable, and therefore could set a bad example for other young people. He had quoted the Bible from the gospel of Paul: "Refrain from giving the appearance of evil." But I had known I was innocent then, just as I knew it now.

The waiter came with our food, and as soon as he left our table, Hortense softened. She looked at me kindly as she continued, "Dean, I have become very fond of you, and I'm aware of your struggle to pay back your loan to our office in Atlanta. I know how you tried so desperately to have money to send your parents. And I will never forget how heartbroken you were when your grandmother died."

Maybe because of her expression of fondness for me, and her mention of my Grandma, I opened up and told Hortense everything that had happened since Jerry's white Cadillac bumped into me. After spilling it all out, I felt as if I was making up a fairy tale and didn't expect her to believe me.

"Wow, what a story!" she said, at first looking happy for me. Quickly, however, her expression became worried again, and I sensed the need to defend myself.

"Though I'm still concerned about this wealthy guy. Have you told your mother?"

"No, because I know she would get sick with worry."

"Yes, your mother would be deeply upset, considering the possible motives of this man."

At this point I was certain that Hortense actually was just being nosy and maybe more than a little jealous. The Appalachian expression, "When you've got nothing, nobody is jealous of you," came to mind. Hortense's insinuations brought out a little of my well-earned survival instincts, and I spoke curtly.

"How could my mother know to advise me about six-place silver settings and the rules rich people have? Mommy would never have considered the likelihood of me being in such an environment as I am now. The knowledge to give me advice on this kind of life would have been as foreign to her as teaching me proper etiquette for dining on the moon!"

165

Soon we asked for the check. I rushed to grab it, and after a discussion about who would pay, I won and paid for our lunch. That was the end of my lunches with Hortense, since I never again accepted her invitations.

Just after five, I left the office and went to the bench Jerry and I had agreed on earlier. I propped myself carefully on the back of the bench, since the seat was dusty. I was again enjoying the refreshing breeze that had always caressed my weary-tired face muscles, as I had waited for Tom to bring me to the bar on his way home.

While enjoying the colorful birds flying up into the trees and alighting on the grass, I had a troubling thought: had I suddenly gotten so involved in looking pretty and proudly showing off my new attire that I was missing the best things in life, like these birds and flowers? I decided that this creature moving timidly around a little dust was not really me, and I would brush that dust off the bench and sit anyway. Just as I started to sit, however, Jerry's car appeared at the curb, and I broke into a run to enter the door he held open for me. There I slid onto the fine leather seat, ready for another adventure in my new world. That moment of deciding I needed to ground myself had swiftly passed. I concluded, like Scarlett O'Hara in *Gone with the Wind*, "I'll think of that tomorrow."

As we cruised down Biscayne Boulevard, Jerry described the Post and Paddock restaurant, where we were heading to meet Ed Sullivan and his wife.

"It's a popular hang-out, especially for the entertainers performing in the best clubs during the winter season. I would so enjoy taking you to all of the best restaurants and nightclubs here."

"I'd love that," I said, and his face lit up with that infectious smile.

"I like your enthusiasm, Dean. It's so refreshing. Most women I see are so blasé, and act as if they're bored until they have a couple rounds of cocktails, and you don't even drink! I am proud of you and I know you're heading toward a bright future."

"I'm already there!"

The salty breeze blew in the windows and a pink-orange sunset softly lit the evening as the Cadillac sailed along. Jerry's relaxed manner and praise made me feel safe and happy.

I have often thought about how Jerry had such sensitivity and insight into any situation. He knew how to make each person feel comfortable. Years later, I concluded that this was one of the reasons he had so many sincere friends. Once I too came to know those friends, I was in awe of the dazzling array of them. Jerry was close to entertainers, shop owners, government officials, ordinary workmen, businessmen, and the blueblood owners of racehorses.

On our way to the restaurant, Jerry started to talk about his college years, when he had worked for Alfred Vanderbilt's mother, keeping books for her racing stables. A year or so after college, he had accepted a job for the American Totalisator Company.

"That's how I entered the field of thoroughbred racing, and I have thoroughly enjoyed an exciting life, even though it has not been without challenges at times."

The mention of thoroughbreds caused me to remember, with a pang of homesickness, the old dilapidated barn where John and Gene, our faithful work mules, had lived, before we moved to the bigger farm in Ellijay. Their shaggy, ungroomed hair reflected my dad's demanding schedule. He was always in such a rush to get the mules out to the fields because he had his mental antennae always alert to possible weather conditions. As I listened to Jerry, I could hear my dad's words: "This may be the last good weather day to work, since the past couple of days, I have heard the east winds blowing in from that old Atlantic, and that's a pretty sure sign we could be in for a couple of weeks of solid rain." Grooming Gene and John had to wait, although most always, as Daddy walked behind the plow to pick up the reins and give the mules the command to start moving, he gave each one's butt an affectionate pat.

At the traffic light, as if he had heard me thinking about Daddy and our hard-working mules, Jerry paused and gave me a rueful smile.

"I must say, Dean, that during your young life you have met and managed to overcome many more difficult hurdles than I."

Soon we arrived at the Post and Paddock, where an awning stretched out over brick steps. The balmy, salty ocean air mixed with Jerry's "wealthy people perfume" as he stood and handed his keys to the valet. These fragrances, and this view of Jerry shaking hands with the young man and handing him the car keys, sent a glow through my entire being much more powerful than any champagne.

As I walked toward the entrance, though, a sense of panic hit me. I had felt so contented, talking with Jerry in the car, yet I couldn't believe I was about to meet Ed Sullivan. *The Ed Sullivan Show* was one of the most popular variety shows on T.V. -- a showcase for celebrities, including both well-known and new musicians and comedians. Everyone in the country knew who Ed Sullivan was.

Jerry squeezed my shoulder, and somehow his strength and confidence made me feel calmer. Before I knew it, my steps came into sync with his, and we walked up the stairs and into the Post and Paddock together. The thought flashed through my mind that I could now benefit from all that rehearsing of Scarlett O'Hara's movements I had done on the rough boards of our mountain shack. How would these close friends of Jerry's feel about me, though?

Jerry touched my shoulder and spoke into my ear. "You will be the most beautiful young woman here." Instantly I felt better.

Some years later I commented to Jerry about how nervous I had felt that night, right before he had introduced me to the Sullivans. I will never forget his response.

"Dean, dear, there is a saying and it goes something like this: 'If one has a heart overflowing with love, such an individual is welcome at the table of kings.' You certainly have that precious quality in abundance. Ed and Sylvia embraced you from the start."

A young man holding menus against his chest smiled as he extended his hand to Jerry and bowed slightly toward me.

"Mr. Brady, it's so good to see you. Mr. and Mrs. Sullivan arrived a few minutes ago." "Adam, it's good to see you again."

Jerry and I started to follow Adam through the dimly lighted foyer. For a moment, my shyness turned into panic. Fine perfumes floated in the atmosphere, but instead of giving me a thrill, they made me feel nauseous.

It was then that I saw Libby. She had just entered the restaurant with a sleek-haired, wealthy gentleman, and was handing her mink stole over to the hat-check lady in the cloak room. Luckily for me, Jerry and I had no wraps, so we avoided bumping into Libby. It was a close call; because I did not wish to let Jerry know I had been a bar fly at that rough bar. I knew Libby had worked for years as a paid escort, in addition to her bar job, and for the first time it hit me that Jerry could well have met her at parties. Remembering how kindly dear Libby had treated me in the bar, I felt lousy to snub her, yet I couldn't help myself. I felt too vulnerable in my new world with Jerry.

As we approached our table, Sylvia and Ed got to their feet and greeted us enthusiastically. My first thought was how pink Ed's face looked. I had seen him many times through the flickering spots that we called "snow" on black and white television screens. Now

170

his face was very animated and his blue eyes sparkled in his startlingly real face. After Jerry introduced us, Ed hugged me. Then Sylvia gave me a big, warm hug as she graciously took my hand and indicated my place at the table, next to her on the cushioned booth side.

In a warm, low voice, she said, "We'll let the men sit on the side of the table that has the chairs."

As soon as I was seated, Sylvia let her arm rest a few seconds on my shoulder. Her touch sent a flash of relief through my body, like a strike of lightning accompanied with a thunderous boom of joy. For a few seconds my mind went back to the conversation with Hortense earlier that day, when I had listened to her unkind predictions about my relationship with Jerry. To my surprise, I felt my heart open to a feeling of sympathy for Hortense and all the Hortenses of the world, who are so ready to snuff out the magic of dreams.

From the moment Sylvia and I sat close together, her hand cupped over mine, the conversation flowed and all the tension melted from my body. Her hands, I noticed, were big and strong, with large joints, in contrast to her slim body. They looked even larger than my mother's work-worn hands. I could not have dreamed how those warm hands of hers would hold mine and comfort me in future years, when the most painful of all struggles enveloped me.

Much of Ed and Jerry's conversation was typical of all good

171

friends, as they shared memories of being kids together in Yonkers. Sylvia asked me questions about my childhood in Georgia. She mentioned that she would like to visit that state. Then she said she knew an inspiring young man, who would reach great heights.

"His name is Martin Luther King."

"Yes, I've been hearing about him," I said. "And I am very proud that, as a child, I walked barefoot on the same red Georgia clay as he did, although I didn't know him."

Hearing me say this, Ed smiled that huge smile, so well-known over the world through his television show. He seemed to appreciate my word picture.

During dinner, many people asked Ed for his autograph or simply came by to say hello. At the end of the evening, Jerry and I agreed to join Ed and Sylvia again soon for the opening of Frank Sinatra and the Rat Pack at the Fontainebleau. We also promised to look for a new date in our calendars for a cruise to Nassau, since our first plan had fallen through.

"Have you ever been on the ocean, Dean?" Ed asked.

"No, but I'd love that one day," I said. "I think it must be wonderful."

That night, I began to see everybody and everything through rose-colored glasses, and that rosy tint stayed with me for many years. From my first glorious meeting with Jerry, everything in my life and the life of my family changed, resulting in much prosperity and good.

As Ed and Sylvia drove home to their suite at the Fontainebleau Hotel that evening, they stopped by Jerry's home and placed a note in his box. Here is what it said: "Jerry, Dean is a thoroughly nice girl. Ed and Sylvia."

Years later, I would sit in the audience watching Elvis Presley make his first television appearance on *The Ed Sullivan Show*. After the thunderous applause for Elvis, Ed came on stage and waved his arm in the direction of this charismatic young singer, who made girls all over the nation swoon. As Elvis bowed to the excited audience, Ed said with his usual million-dollar smile, "Elvis is a thoroughly nice boy!"

I still feel a thrill when I remember that I shared the same compliment Ed Sullivan gave to that nice boy Elvis!

LUAU BOOSTER — Drinks are king size at Luau Restaurant as demonstrated by comedian Phil Silvers (far left) who provided plenty of off-cuff after dinner entertainment for (left to right) Danny Arnstein, New York Yellow Cab owner; Dean- Warren, of Miami Beach, and Jerry Brady of American Totalisator Co. in New York. Silvers is vacationing at the Roney Plaza for a few days before returning to New York and his CBS television show.

Figure 5: … Just After We Met …

12: A Glamorous Life

One day soon after meeting the Sullivans, I felt that my movements in the insurance office, as I shuffled papers and files, were as rhythmic and joyous as the performances of young celebrities and dancers on Dick Clark's American Bandstand, the most popular afternoon television show of the 1950's.

As I opened the metal file drawers in my boss's office and found the right spot for each manila folder, I marveled about these past few days with Jerry and his friends. I wished I could shout to the rooftops about my good luck, instead of simply smiling and saying hello to my fellow office workers. Since before my early teenage years, I had read about the sophisticated members of the cafe society described in the Hollywood gossip columns pasted to our cabin walls. Once I had come to Miami Beach, I had pored over the society pages of the *Miami Herald* and the *Miami Daily News,* since my boss subscribed to both the morning and the afternoon city newspapers. I had constantly dreamed that I would soon be part of that social world. Now, because of Jerry, I had somehow catapulted right into the heart of it.

Jerry, of course, was older than the young people dancing on American Bandstand or filling the cafes and nightclubs of Miami, and as I went through my day at the insurance office, I started to understand that his position in life was part of what appealed to me most. Picturing his elegant streaks of grey hair and his calm confidence, I realized I was falling in love with a perfect example of a man who was already on top of the best kind of life. He had become so attractive to me because the changeable and unsure years were behind him. As I looked ahead to more evenings together, it struck me that it was Jerry's cultured, stable, happy life, with good friends, that I now hoped to share, more than the superficial lifestyles of young celebrities splashed all over the magazines.

As I continued to file papers in the cabinets behind my boss's desk, Hortense flung open the door to his office. She had come in from the typing pool to place a batch of letters and papers on Mr. Hardeman's desk. Usually when she entered, she seemed too busy to speak, but today she looked me up and down.

"I must say, Dean, you still do have the fanciest clothes!"

She stood in front of me for a moment, with a curious and insinuating look, as if she could say a lot more given half a chance, but I just said, "Thank you, Hortense," and turned my back on her. She slammed the door behind her in her usual brusque manner.

In the silence after she left, I looked out the window onto Biscayne Boulevard, with its rows of huge palm trees on each side. The ones nearest to the Bay were making dancing shadows on the water, as the wind shook their long draping leaves.

My mind flew back to the day when I had first come to this office. Anxious and hungry, I had not been at all sure Mr. Hardeman would hire me, because file clerks were a dime a dozen. I felt hopeful that my boss in Atlanta had sent a good word for me along with the papers, but realistically I knew that this hopefulness was mostly based on the fact that I owed the Atlanta office $400.00. I worried that this Miami office would hire me simply in order to make sure I paid the company back, out of my paycheck.

Now so much had changed. I had a champion, in Jerry, and a dozen dresses in my very own closet, in my own apartment. No longer would I have to worry about having only a few dollars in my purse, and counting my pennies as I stood at a lunch counter. Maybe I would be able to quit this job, and never wonder again about what Mr. Hardeman or Hortense or anyone thought of me. Maybe Jerry would ask me to marry him, and I could be happy with him forever.

As I gazed out of the large second floor window, I realized that I couldn't remember ever seeing that huge colorful Bay as clearly as this. The banks along the water were abundantly filled with tall slender palm trees, just as the water was filled with yachts and small boats. The sun seemed to be making a pathway of light across the shimmering Bay straight to my window, while the breeze from the open window played with my silk lavender scarf, allowing it to give me a soft pat on my face with the same touch as Jerry's hand.

I turned away from the window. I told myself firmly that I had to put a halt to such daydreaming about marriage, because I realized that such a goal could not be reached. How could I hope to

177

share Jerry's life with him? What made me think this could even be possible? Why not be sensible and enjoy the grandeur of just being with him for as long as this could last?

Moving closer to Mr. Hardeman's desk to pick up more papers to file, I stumbled over his trash can and simultaneously overturned a vase of violets. Just the day before, he had been caressing the violets and telling me, "These are from my son Jordan. He picked them from our back yard." His smile had been broad and his eyes sparkling.

"In my opinion, Jordan is a very lucky boy," I had said.

Now I made haste to clean up the mess I had made. Luckily, the little glass vase hadn't broken, and still had some water in it, so I carefully gathered the violets and placed them into the vase. I smiled to myself, thinking about how Colleen and I used to pick wildflowers and bring them home to Mommy and Grandma. As I started to catch up with my office tasks, I reminded myself that sometimes the impossible could become possible. At certain important moments in my young life, after all, my dreamy prayerful thoughts had come true, even though from a sensible point of view other people might have urged me to give up hope. As Emerson said, "Once you make a decision, the universe conspires to make it happen."

Practically skipping through the insurance office, with my left hand pressing a number of files against my breast, I commenced to count on the fingers of my right hand some of those instances when impossible dreams had come true. First, Mother did recover from that awful sickness, and later so did Daddy get well when Mr. Hagan entered our lives and kindly saw to it that he could get medical care. The shiny red tractor too had become a reality. I had decided to buy it for Daddy, and I had made this happen. When I was little, it had looked as if we would surely lose our home from overdue property taxes, and like manna in Moses's day, Mrs. Leach's jelly money had saved us from the taxman. And no dream come true had meant more to my young mind, hungry to learn, than the entrance of Mr. Hagan into our life. In giving my family a chance to work on his chicken farm, and then to move into his farmhouse, he had furnished Colleen and me with the opportunity to finish high school.

My counting of blessings was interrupted as I glimpsed a picture of the Sullivans on the front page of the *Miami Herald*. The photo showed them exiting the Post and Paddock restaurant. I realized that this photo must have been taken just after they had said goodbye to Jerry and me. We had lingered in our booth awhile, chatting with other friends. Looking at the picture made the events of the Post and Paddock seem like concrete facts rather than a magnificent dream. I made a note to come back by Mr. Hardeman's office and bring the newspaper home with me, because I knew he had a habit of discarding his daily papers each afternoon. I thought how surprised Mommy and Daddy would be when I told them I had been just inside that restaurant in the photo, where Jerry and I had dined with so many famous people, including the Ed Sullivans.

I still felt too cautious to tell my parents much about Jerry, however. I wanted to make sure first that this relationship would continue. I would be glad when the telephone man in Ellijay installed the telephone Jerry had ordered for my parents. Jerry had given the Ellijay Telephone Company my new number, and Mommy and Daddy were to call me as soon as their phone was installed. I knew they were as excited as I was about this, and although I felt a little guilty letting them think I had paid for this new phone, I tried to look on the bright side and simply be happy for us all, and grateful to Jerry.

As I cleared the last papers and said goodbye to my co-workers, a light-hearted feeling cheered me that this might be the day my parents would ring me at my apartment. The following moment, though, I remembered that I wouldn't be home, because Jerry and I would be heading straight to his friend Danny Arnstein's house. I hoped Mommy and Daddy would receive their new phone the next day, so I could call them then, and tell them about meeting Danny Arnstein. He sounded like someone who had once been very poor, and I felt that my parents would like to hear his story.

Jerry had told me, "Danny's young life reminds me of yours, Dean, in that he worked so hard, with two jobs, to get money to buy his first cab. Now he's a taxi tycoon, with millions of dollars and a fleet of yellow cabs in Chicago and New York."

Apparently Danny had been raised in the slums of Chicago. He and his mother had lived alone and struggled to survive. She had taken in laundry for a living, while Danny had spent his nights sleeping in his cab, waiting for customers who needed to get somewhere before dawn, when Danny had to get to his day job.

I had laughed when Jerry described the way Danny's taxis showed a picture of his little dog Wags on the sides. Wags had been a loyal companion, who had kept Danny company in the early days, sitting right up in the front seat with him.

As I hopped into Jerry's car after work, he said, "Following dinner at Danny's, we'll go back to our apartments and dress in evening clothes for the Rat Pack show. You'll meet most everyone at Danny's, since his home is a hangout for a lot of entertainers."

He mentioned that Senator Lyndon B. Johnson's attorney Eddie Weisel and Eddie's wife Alice would be there that evening, which meant we were sure to have matzo ball soup for our first course.

"Eddie declares that Danny's cook, Linda, makes the best matzo ball soup in the world."

I wondered what this soup would be like. It sounded more homemade than the food I had been enjoying in fancy restaurants. What would a soup be like, with some kind of balls floating in it? For a moment I thought back to my Grandma's soups, and felt a twinge of homesickness. On cold winter days, our house would be filled with the fragrance of her bean soup bubbling on the stove, and her cornbread baking in the oven.

Coming into Danny's long driveway, I realized that his property bordered the Oceanside Park where I had rehearsed my plan to walk into the waves. Shivering, I could easily see the spot where I had stood in the sand firming up my plans. Listening to Jerry's warm voice, I pressed my high heels firmly against the floorboard, feeling a rush of gratitude for this savior beside me.

Jerry stopped the engine in front of a big mansion and said, "Welcome to Danny's Hideaway, as we affectionately refer to it. In a moment I hope to introduce you to the man himself. You know, he owns my favorite steakhouse in New York City, Danny's Hideaway."

I smiled at Jerry and then looked out the window. That was when I gasped, because I saw someone I could never have hoped to see in real life, standing right beside a plump, short palm tree in Danny's garden. I almost rubbed my eyes to clear them, but it was true: there he was -- the skinny legend with the glorious voice -- Frank Sinatra!

For a second, I had the urge to act like a typical young fan, rushing out of the car and straight ahead to crash the singer's solitude on this magical moonlit night. Just as quickly as the teenage urge seized me, though, it floated away into the air, as Jerry opened the door on my side of the Cadillac. With a naturalness I did not actually feel, I walked with dignity toward the skinny man by the palm tree, to be properly introduced. And for many years thereafter I was grateful for the control that suddenly took hold and allowed me to amble over in such a leisurely way with Jerry, who, as I would soon find out, had been a friend of Frank Sinatra's for years. In conversations in the following weeks, Frank would tell me how Jerry's solid position in the thoroughbred racing world had been an inspiration and firm help to him as he had maneuvered his way through many challenging life situations.

Talking with the heartthrob of the nation, "Old Blue Eyes," I could see how very blue indeed his eyes were, lit by the string of bright lights hugging the palm tree he stood beside. After our friendly conversation with Frank, Jerry said to him, "See you inside!" and he guided me through the crowd of guests, who were laughing and talking in groups on the lawn.

"Now I'd like to introduce you to Gene Mori," Jerry said, "owner of the Hialeah Race Track, one of the best racing tracks in the world."

A dapper man, a head shorter than Jerry, graciously shook my hand, smiling and bowing.

"Miss Warren, a pleasure to meet you! Jerry tells me you're from Atlanta, one of my favorite cities."

Two swift thoughts flew into my mind: a feeling of pleasure that Jerry had been talking about me with his friend, and a sudden uncomfortable snapshot of my own struggling time in Atlanta, and how it must have contrasted sharply with the life of Gene Mori and his friends.

"It's a thrill meeting you, Mr. Mori," I said. "Ever since I moved here, I've been reading about you and Hialeah Race Track."

I couldn't help blushing, because the truth was, I hadn't actually read about Hialeah. This racecourse had been a major subject of conversation at the bar where I had worked as a bar fly.

Our conversation was interrupted by an outpouring of applause for a young singing group I didn't know -- two young men and a woman with long blonde hair. Years later, listening to Peter, Paul and Mary sing, I realized they were the same singers I had glimpsed at that first party at Danny Arnstein's.

Soon Jerry introduced me to a short, bald man, who greeted me with a big smile and a firm handshake.

"Dean, I would like you to meet Eddie Weisel, personal attorney to Senator Lyndon Johnson."

Shaking Eddie's hand, I remembered what Jerry had said about the matzo ball soup, and I looked around, wondering if this would be our first course. Within the hour, this soup was indeed served, as all of us sat at tables inside Danny's house, covered with white tablecloths and candles. I loved the soup, yet I silently concluded that, scrumptious though this famous dish was, it was not nearly as good as Grandma's chicken soup, created after she had killed and dressed a chicken from our yard and simmered it for hours on that old black wood stove.

Over the next ten years, Eddie Weisel and his wife Alice would become close friends, and Jerry and I would often visit them, both in Miami and in their Central Park South home in New York. Sometimes it would be just the four of us. Other times we would be joined by Phil Silvers, who was the rowdy Sergeant Bilco in a beloved and zany television comedy, or Milton Berle. Because Danny could see it was so much fun for me, he most always seated me between Jerry and one or another exciting show business personality. In addition to Frank Sinatra, entertainers like Tony Bennett and Dean Martin were often our dinner partners. In fact, the Rat Pack -- including Dean Martin, Frank Sinatra, Joey Bishop, and Sammy Davis, Jr. -- all became a familiar part of my world with Jerry.

For all of these parties and shows, I was now a member of this glittering new crowd, which felt like family. I found it was actually okay to drink my champagne and wine, instead of discreetly getting rid of alcohol, as I had had to do when I was a bar girl. Now I was privileged to live in a world both safe and thrilling.

At that first dinner party at Danny's, Jerry and I left the merriment to go outside into the garden, where we sat together in a single beach lounge chair. Just as Jerry's embrace pulled me closer to his muscular body, the large door opened and one of Danny's housekeepers called loudly to Jerry, above the music and laughter vibrating inside.

"Mr. Brady, Mr. Sullivan is on the phone."

"Thank you, Mary Louise," Jerry called back.

Jerry turned to me and said gently, "Let's go in now."

"Oh Jerry, you go ahead. I really wish to stay here alone and take time to digest the magic of my new life."

Jerry's eyes registered a touch of surprise, but also a sincere effort to understand me. His smile looked otherworldly in the moonlight. He touched my shoulder and kissed the top of my head before going inside.

After he left, I stayed in the beach chair, watching the waves glistening in the moonlight. I realized that the ocean looked so friendly to me now. Remembering my lifelong yearning to write a book, I promised myself that someday I would write about my experiences, with the hope of encouraging some lost soul who might be rehearsing a plan to end her life, just as I had done before Jerry's car bumped into me so close to this spot.

Soon after our first joyful weeks together, I decided to tell Jerry about the money I still owed to my insurance company, which I had used for the abortion in Atlanta. The company had been taking a small amount out of my paychecks each month, and yet I still owed over $250.00 after two and a half years of payments. I worried about telling Jerry both about this debt and about the reason for it, afraid that he would experience profound distaste about my brief affair with the married man and all the entanglement from that. I worried more because, although Jerry didn't practice Catholicism, he was brought up a strict Catholic. Still, I felt that I owed it to Jerry to be honest about my past. I had come to the point where I didn't want to have any secrets from him. If we were to continue in our relationship, he had to know the whole truth.

One night after we had had dinner in his home, I finally got up the nerve to tell him. He placed his warm, caring arm around my shoulders and then, after his habitual soft, sweet pats, he arose to go to his desk. He opened the middle drawer, pulled out his checkbook, and asked simply, "How much is the balance?"

"A little more than $250.00."

Jerry nodded and bent over the desk, writing out a check. When he showed it to me with a shy smile, I realized that the check was for $1,000.00.

"This is a bit more for all the worries you've had the past year."

I jumped up, flushed with surprise, gratitude, and a whirl of other emotions I couldn't quite name. All the difficulties of the past few years swirled inside me: my awful marriage, the frightening abortion, my first two hardworking years in Miami, my period of homelessness at the boarding house, and my intention to drown in the ocean. How could all of that have led to this moment? I started to cry as I walked over to the window facing the entrance to the public beach across Collins Avenue, where I had first met Jerry. I could not believe how lucky I had been to meet this large-hearted

187

man. It struck me more powerfully than ever before, that he was not only a Prince in appearance, but in soul.

Jerry came to stand beside me. His face was filled with sadness and affection as he lifted my chin, looked into my eyes, and said, "I don't know how a young lady could have endured all the pain you have been forced to suffer."

He gently gave me the check, and then he brushed his hands briskly up and down, saying, "Now that is over. The end of a bad memory!"

With his strong arms, he lifted me in the direction of the ceiling as if to lift me above all the sad thoughts, and cheerfully added, "Now let's have a nice walk in the soft, salty air to Pumperniks. The breezes are healing and a hot chocolate would be nourishing."

Soon we were sitting cozily in our corner booth, feeling closer to each other than ever before.

13: On the Yacht with my Prince

One special evening, that first spring with Jerry, still rings clearly in my memory, like a favorite song. Our yacht cruise to Nassau was finally about to happen. On the spur of the moment, Jerry and I would sail with Ed and Sylvia, Ben and Joan Gaines, one hundred and eighty miles across the glittering ocean to that beautiful island, where we would swim, shop and go to restaurants together. I had often viewed the large yachts sailing near the coast of Miami Beach, but I had never dreamed I would ever be on one.

Although all of us had hoped to go on our cruise in January, it had turned out to be a few months before the three busy couples could coordinate plans. Now in April, the Sullivans were back in Miami Beach and the date set for us to leave would be the following day.

Jerry had surprised me that morning by telephoning me at the insurance company. Since his business ethics were as impeccable as his social grace, he was usually careful not to call me at work.

"Dean, would it be possible for you to get a few days off immediately for us to take our mini vacation in Nassau, even starting tomorrow morning?"

I felt like dancing right in the office.

"Yes! I'll ask my boss," I said, smiling as I held the receiver.

189

"Shall I go over to your place and pack your bag for you? Then we'll be all set, and we can enjoy our evening tonight."

I thanked him, and gave him a list of all the items I'd like to bring on the cruise.

Mr. Hardeman generously gave me permission to have those days off, and at five o'clock, when Jerry drove up to the bench just outside the insurance company, I gleefully told him the good news as I glided next to him in the convertible.

"That's wonderful! I've got you all packed. Shall we go to our usual place for dinner?" he asked, meaning Pumperniks.

"I'd love it," I said, my happiness bubbling up like champagne.

We had a lovely dinner sitting close together at Pumperniks in the corner window booth, which the staff had named "Mr. Brady's table." I had discovered that this booth had been special to him for many years, especially because he had often been alone. He told me how, on a lunch break, or on weekend mornings, he had always found it a pleasant and relaxing pastime to glance out the nearby open window and see happy vacationers as they walked down Collins Avenue in the brilliant sun.

Once we had settled into our booth, Jerry laughingly said, "You know my personal relationship with this booth."

"This booth will always be precious to me, because it was the first place you took me, after you rescued me. I will always remember how delicious that breakfast was!"

He reached over and gave my hand a warm squeeze. "I wonder if you will like a little plan for tonight that I have been thinking about all day."

Just then the waiter came for our order. I quickly ordered a Reuben sandwich on rye bread, since it was the first thing that came to mind. I was so eager to hear what Jerry had been thinking that I couldn't bother with the menu.

Once the waiter had left, Jerry said, "I thought it might be fun, since we already have our bags packed, if we take our luggage to the yacht." He smiled, and with a shy glance added, "You and I could actually spend the night there, so you might get used to the feel of being in bedrooms on a yacht, before we leave tomorrow."

His use of the word "bedrooms" in the plural sent a flicker of disappointment into my heart. However, he hadn't given me any reason to assume I would get to sleep with him.

I shrugged this disappointment off, saying, "I would be thrilled to stay on the yacht with you tonight, Jerry."

He grinned. "Well, that's settled then."

Just at sundown, we parked on Biscayne Bay at the dock.

"Isn't this a marvelous evening?" Jerry asked, as he lightly touched my arm to guide me to the yacht.

His "marvelous" comment reminded me of Mrs. Leach, the Coca Cola lady, who often told my Mommy and Daddy how marvelous I was, while in the next sentence she'd be speaking about the wonderful jelly they had made and brought her. Now the soft,

191

salty ocean breeze, mixing with that "rich person smell" of Jerry's, made me a bit giddy in the head. I nodded happily, feeling too "marvelous" to utter words.

Once inside the yacht, I felt as if I were truly in a fairy tale and a wand had brought forth magic. I was surprised by how home-like this yacht felt. Art hung on the walls, and two plush beige sofas sat together, with matching stuffed chairs. One side of the long living room held a liquor cabinet and a small fridge. Jerry looked at me hesitantly.

"Would you like me to mix you a drink?" he asked.

I laughed. "Jerry, you know I don't drink!"

Jerry smiled broadly as he gave a little slap to his forehead.

"Of course! I forgot. I'm sorry, Dean. It's so refreshing to me that you're like me on that point."

Most of Jerry's friends enjoyed relaxing with a mixed drink. He hardly drank at all, though -- perhaps a sherry once in a while before dinner.

"I guess it's natural for me to lean toward the healthy lifestyle," he said, "because of how hard I worked to get a baseball scholarship. I just got in the habit."

I loved that story about Jerry. From Yonkers High School, he had won a scholarship to the University of Pittsburgh.

"Of course, it didn't hurt my chances for a scholarship that my best high school buddy was little Eddie Sullivan, the famous sports editor of our mighty high school newspaper!" Jerry laughed and winked at me.

I laughed too, thinking of a young Ed, making his way up in the world of Yonkers.

"So you already knew an important person back then."

"Yes!" he said, grinning. "Did I ever tell you," he added, "after college I had a year with the Pittsburgh Pirates baseball team?"

"You did?!" I loved learning new, surprising information like this. I especially enjoyed glimpses of Jerry's earlier life, because he hardly ever shared such facts about his accomplishments.

Jerry looked a touch embarrassed, though, as if he thought he was talking too much about himself. Lightly touching my arm, he pointed to the door leading outside to the terrace deck, and we walked outside together, hand in hand. The deck sofa was covered in a casual bright fabric designed with red roses and large green leaves. The material looked strongly woven, giving the appearance of being able to stand an onslaught of rain.

Jerry started to sit beside me, though a sudden thought prompted him to say as enthusiastically as a paid promoter of Florida orange juice, "I'm going back inside to bring us a couple of glasses of that fresh, healthy orange juice."

By now, the huge Miami moon shone down almost as brightly as sunlight. The yacht sat majestically poised on the shimmering moonlit water as we sat together, sipping our orange juice. During those magical evening hours, I kept gazing at the reflection of the moon's silver pathway in the calm water. I felt so enveloped in love, with Jerry's warm, vibrant breath lightly ruffling my hair, and seeming to become a shared breath between us. At one point, when I moved to face Jerry, before my eyes a halo of light appeared around his head, and stayed visible for a few astonishing seconds. I did not say anything to Jerry about this vision -- I thought he might laugh -- though it was such a blissful moment, and I still cherish this special memory.

A year later, while we were dining with Sylvia and Ed at Henry Soule's Pavillon in New York City, I told them the story about that halo. Jerry blushed, while Ed and Sylvia threw back their heads and laughed. Ed could not seem to stop. With both hands holding his napkin over his mouth, his laughing continued and tears welled up in his eyes. Senator Jack and his wife Jackie Kennedy looked over at us and smiled. And for years after that, whenever we were together, Ed would tease me, saying, "Dean, have you seen that halo over Jerry's head lately?"

"It's still there," I always said with a big smile, and it still *was* there in continuing intensity through all the years I lived with Jerry.

On the yacht deck that April evening, Jerry and I watched other yachts and commercial cruise ships moving at a distance on Biscayne Bay. I started asking Jerry about our plans for the trip to Nassau. Jerry shifted uncomfortably on our sofa and cleared his throat.

"Well, Dean, I am sorry to tell you, but I just discovered this afternoon that there's a chance I may not be able to come with you tomorrow."

I sat up and looked closely at Jerry. Could it be something wrong with his health, or a family problem?

"What is it?" I asked, trying to sound calm.

"Well, I got a call today about a major problem that's developed with our equipment at Hialeah." He took my hands and held them in his. "I'm hoping it will all be ironed out by the time we start to sail tomorrow. But if I can't join you, I want you to please go anyway. It's a great little group, with only Joan and Ben and the Sullivans. Perhaps I will be able to fly out to Nassau for the last day or so."

I sat upright. Raising my voice, I said, "Oh no, if you can't go I won't go either. I'd rather be here with you."

"Are you sure?" he asked, as I positioned myself back, snuggling closer to him.

He let his arm drop from the back of the sofa and tighten briefly around my shoulders, quickly placing it again on the sofa. I felt that all this dreamy joy flooding my being was too good to be true, and I thought my heart might just stop beating.

After one more brief squeeze of my shoulder, Jerry said rather briskly, "We'd best go inside and get ready for bed."

Walking down the yacht's hallway, I tried to identify the

195

luscious smells, which mixed with Jerry's cologne and the Bay air. I could detect the lemon fragrance of polished wood and the crisp, tantalizing scent of linens freshly washed and ironed. For one instant, the scent of my Mommy's herb garden came to me, filled with a mixture of oregano, lemon verbena, and mint, and a touch of the scrub pines nearby, all of it heating up in the sunshine of Georgia.

"When we arrived," Jerry said, "I meant to show you the four bedrooms, but I got distracted." Pointing to the left of the hallway, he said, "This first bedroom will be where Sylvia and Ed sleep, and the second one will be Joan and Ben's." Pointing to the right, he said, "The first bedroom here is yours and the next one down is mine."

Jerry walked into my bedroom ahead of me and turned on the lights.

"I hope you sleep well, Dean, and if you need anything, you know where I am. There's a nightlight on in the hall."

He placed his arm around my shoulders, gave me three familiar soft pats, and smiled as he left my room.

I thought, this surely is the bedroom of a princess. Yet I felt keenly disappointed. I wanted to be near that flesh and blood body of Jerry's, and I was frustrated that the full happiness I had hoped for had slipped out of my reach. I felt that the closed door of my room symbolized the turning away from all the joy any human being is capable of experiencing, at least once in a lifetime.

In a state of wistfulness I put on my nightgown and brushed my teeth, turned off the light and got into bed. At first, I felt comforted by the sound of the waves lapping against the yacht, and the gentle movements of the boat on the water. A few moments later, however, my isolation overwhelmed me, and I tossed the sweet-smelling covers off, jumped out of bed, leaped down the hall and burst into Jerry's room. In the darkness, I followed his sexy smell, right toward his bed.

Touching Jerry's chest in the dark, I said, "I don't want to be in that bed. I want to be here with you!"

He raised the covers and I crawled in beside him.

"Oh Dean, you're such a baby." His muffled voice came from my smothering grasp of his face between my breasts.

"I'm not a baby!" I practically yelled, "and I'll show you!"

The next morning, Jerry drove us back to his villa. I had the day off, because of the plans for the cruise. As he got ready to go to his office, he said, "How about if you relax here today, and I take you home tonight, after dinner at Pumperniks?" His eyes twinkled. "Or maybe you could just spend the night here?"

"How could I refuse an offer that promises to be like last night?"

He gave a big laugh and said, "You know you are a bit wicked, Dean!"

Could I be the same person who had declared a few months

earlier that I never wanted another man to touch me? As I gave Jerry an ardent hug and kiss, I thought happily that I was ready to revise such declarations now.

May was fast approaching. According to Jerry's yearly schedule, he would leave Miami Beach in mid-May to spend the summer traveling and living in his apartment at the Delmonico Hotel in New York.

One day soon after our "cruise," Jerry invited me to join him in New York that summer. I accepted with joy, promising that I would come up to the city after I spent the rest of May, June, and July in Georgia, visiting my Mom and Dad. Jerry and I decided that during my birthday month of August, I would visit him in New York.

I told my boss that I would be in Georgia for three months, and then in New York visiting Jerry. I smiled, feeling shy about telling him too much, yet I had a feeling that Mr. Hardeman understood. He had become fond of Jerry that spring, and felt grateful for Jerry's kindness in giving him box seats at the race track on many occasions.

"To be honest, Mr. Hardeman, I'm not quite sure when I will come back to Miami! So maybe you should give my job to someone else." I smiled self-consciously.

Exuberant with delight, he embraced me and said, "Go, with my blessing! When I met you, Dean, your life was in such a turmoil. Now I have a feeling you're headed toward a fairytale life, and it couldn't happen to a dearer young woman. Enjoy yourself, and stop by at the office whenever you can."

I thanked him and reached for another embrace, this time with my tears dampening his immaculate shirt. He didn't seem to mind at all.

Now my thoughts started to turn toward home, and the people I had loved so deeply since my childhood. What would it be like to be on the mountain now? Although I looked forward to spending the summer in Georgia, I knew I would miss Jerry tremendously. I loved him more and more each day.

PART II

The Glories of the Ritz

14: Summer in Georgia

After four months of life with Jerry in Miami Beach, the day in May came when we had to say goodbye. I would be catching an Eastern Airlines flight to Atlanta, and Jerry would soon fly to New York.

Jerry had asked his friend Alfred Vanderbilt if George, Alfred's chauffeur, could drive me to the airport. During the winter George had driven us to a number of social functions. I liked him very much, since we spoke the same language, Southern -- he was originally from Gainesville, Georgia. He was a distinguished African American Southern gentleman with graying hair. His slender, wiry body, sparkling eyes and soft, slow speech reminded me somewhat of my Dad.

Daddy's telephone call earlier that morning, confirming the time he would pick me up at the Atlanta Airport, had touched my heart, because it made me realize what I could hardly believe was actually happening: in just a few hours, I would be hearing that same slow, warm voice of my Daddy's, cherishing me and expressing pure joy as I gave him and Mommy a big hug. This thought had helped me as I stood by the limousine, embracing Jerry for the last time before August.

Both Daddy and Jerry showed their love quietly and tenderly, without too much emotion. Mommy and I, of course, were more excitable. Mommy's voice on the phone that morning had been shrill with happiness.

"My little Cotton-top, I can't hardly wait until I hug you at the airport!" Her last word was high-pitched with joy, an emotion I shared in full measure.

Cruising along Biscayne Boulevard with George, I had the same thought I'd often had in this luxurious limo: that its interior was the same size as my room in the boarding house had been, without the mildew or brown stains on the ceiling. Looking out the window, I felt my heart speaking a silent thank you to the palm trees along Biscayne Bay. I had learned to love those trees so, and as we sailed past, I fancied that I had an affinity with them: like me, they were always reaching higher for newer and better circumstances. Just as they carried their branches up into the sky with them, I wanted to bring my family along with me on my upward journey.

Jerry had continued to help my family in his quiet way, with a generosity that still amazed me. He had given me the money to buy them a new Ford Fairlane -- the best car they had ever had the chance to own. In the weeks before my flight to Georgia, he had insisted on giving me the money to start remodeling my parents' house over the summer. He hoped Mommy and Daddy could add new rooms, modern appliances, and the comfort of central air conditioning and heating. Jerry refused even to discuss my future repayment of such gifts. Instead, he simply repeated that I had immeasurably enriched his life in more ways than I would ever know. He frequently expressed his philosophy that lots of things were more worthy and important than material objects. Evidently I was one of those worthy and important entities.

My parents never questioned too closely the source of all this money. They appeared to accept the notion that I made quite a good income through my modeling. They trusted their children so absolutely, and knew so little of the ways of the world, that it did not occur to them that Jerry might be the one to offer such extraordinary gifts -- or, if it did occur to them, I had a feeling they brushed off the thought quickly, feeling embarrassed by it. I had told them in phone conversations about Jerry, of course, comparing him favorably to the generous and caring Mr. Hagan. Mommy and Daddy would exclaim, wholeheartedly, "Yes, he really does seem like Mr. Hagan, and we often comment about that."

Sometimes in our phone conversations that spring, however, I had caught a glimmer of my parents' worries about my actual situation. A few times, they hinted at questioning Jerry's motives for his kindness. This subject made me uncomfortable, so I always tried to steer away from it. I couldn't quite understand my relationship with Jerry yet, either, although I did understand my own wishes. I liked my own comparison of Jerry with Mr. Hagan, but I realized my feelings were not as simple or innocent as my girlhood crush on Mr. Hagan. Throughout the winter and early spring, I had felt frustrated waiting for that sexy Jerry to grab me and hug me! It had seemed forever that I had to be satisfied with little pats on my shoulder. Remembering how the neighbors had squashed my relationship with Mr. Hagan, I knew what my family would say if they really understood my feelings for Jerry, and our budding romance.

George ever so smoothly brought the limo to a stop at the airport, and opened the trunk for the porter to load my new blue Samsonite luggage onto the cart. George then came around to help me with my carry-on luggage and escort me to the sidewalk.

Startled, I watched a lady pushing an old grocery cart stuffed with dirty clothes right in front of me. She looked amazingly like my Grandma -- so much so, that I just stared at her, almost believing she *was* my Grandma, come back somehow in this form. The lady had placed a torn blanket over the top of her cart, and had hung a number of worn shopping bags from the sides. Strands of gray hair like my grandmother's dangled down her face, but what really stunned me, as she looked steadily right at me, was how much her piercing eyes reminded me of my Grandma's, as she would gaze into my own eyes after her hard day of dirty work. There was even a brown mole on this woman's left cheek, just like my Grandma's.

Instinctively I lunged forward to hug her, but before I could, George carefully and firmly guided me behind the porter who was pushing my luggage into the airport lobby. Listening to the clang of the shopping cart wheels behind me, I felt stunned and shaken.

Unable to resist the urge to look over my shoulder, I saw that the woman's eyes were still glued on me. I stood still, just gazing at her, and George paused for a moment, surprised and concerned by my behavior. I realized he needed some explanation, since he did not know me all that well.

"That woman looks just like my Grandma!" I exclaimed. My voice must have been loud; since I noticed other people begin to stare at us. "It can't be my grandma, though. She's been dead for seven months."

"Oh, Miss Warren, I'm so sorry," George said. A sense of relief was evident on his face as he realized that the lady pushing the shopping cart wasn't really my Grandma.

As we approached the ticket agent, George said with a broad smile lighting his face, "Now, Miss Warren, you have a lovely vacation in Georgia, and remember, should you need me, you know where to reach me, as one Georgia neighbor might say to another."

Having lightened the mood, he tipped his hat and walked back toward the limo, waving a couple of times before he disappeared through the door.

Once I walked inside the plane, the stewardess smiled and pointed me toward a spacious first-class seat. Since Jerry had purchased my ticket, I had been looking forward to the thrill of being able to enter the plane and turn left to enter the first-class section instead of turning right to find my seat in the coach section, but the thrill I had anticipated did not come. Instead, before I could even reach my seat, I started to cry as I thought about the woman in the airport. I continued to sob in my seat, overcome with fresh, fierce emotions about my grandmother's death. I felt aware that this was the most out of control weeping I had experienced since that time, so many years earlier, when my heart had broken as I watched my mother wrestle with the pain of mastoiditis, and knew there was no money to pay for a doctor.

I could not erase from my mind the picture of that homeless lady, the image of Grandma. I began to realize, even more powerfully than I had on my last visit home, that I would not see Grandma in my family's house -- I would never see her again. In thinking about the blissful months just past, right up until this morning as I said goodbye to Jerry, I pondered the sudden turnaround in my emotions. It came to me that I had been so caught up in my own life's struggles and happiness that I had not truly faced my Grandma's death. I recalled that, during the time I had spent with my parents after her death, I had nurtured and cared for my Mommy during her many deeply depressing days and sleepless nights. She had had frequent outbursts of tears. Focusing on her needs, I had had a difficult time finding a way to do my own mourning.

During the periods when Mommy could handle her grief with a measure of composure, I would walk toward my special rock on the creek bank, a rock shaped somewhat like a chair, where I could be alone and let myself feel the pain of Grandma's death, a reality I had to face. Alas, my rock too was often no comfort, because I would most likely find my strong, tough Daddy sitting on the creek bank pleading with God to take away the awful grief he could not overcome. I would immediately turn back to the house and into the kitchen to make a meal for both of my parents, which would somehow have to take the place of the specially prepared suppers my blessed Grandma had so lovingly served us in those earlier years. Then, once I returned to Miami and discovered that the landlady had left with the money I had trustingly placed in her hands, I had just put my sorrow away, and coped with my shattered world in the boarding house.

My sobs slowed down. As I sat in my comfortable seat on the airplane, gazing at the empty seat next to me, I came to the raw realization that after dreaming in my childhood of gaining plenty of earthly goods for my Grandma, now that they had miraculously come into my life, Grandma was no longer here to enjoy them. Our family's lives throughout history had been founded on unselfish sharing with each other. Here I was, on my own; grateful for all that I had, yet yearning only to be able to have the impossible chance to share it with my Grandma.

Wiping my eyes with a handkerchief, I heard a kind voice float its way to me, as if out of a dark tunnel.

"Is there anything at all I could bring you to make you feel better?"

I looked up to see the young stewardess, bending toward me with a compassionate look on her face. I shook my head as I thanked her. Before I knew it, I had dozed off.

About an hour later something happened that I will always hold close. I awakened with a most peaceful sense that totally took me by surprise. I couldn't believe the calm and clarity that now enveloped me. Listening to the droning jet motor, I tried to awaken more fully, because I thought I might be dreaming. As I let my eyes close again, a picture appeared in my consciousness. It was my Grandma's face, with her Mona Lisa smile, and I knew in that instant that she had taken those loving hands that had so often comforted me, and lifted the curtain of my grief. When my Grandma accomplished a task, she did it thoroughly, and I thanked her now for lifting my heart and soul so completely, and giving me peace.

Looking from the window, I could see the mountains of my youth, where experiences of the deepest and sweetest joy, alternating with worry and pain, formed the patchwork of my years. Scene after scene of my childhood kept playing over in my mind as we made our descent into Atlanta. Overwhelming gratitude flooded my thoughts for all the years I had spent with my family among those trees and hills, growing and being molded into the person I had become at that moment. My sturdy upbringing had surely helped me cope with the difficulties in both Atlanta and Miami, before Jerry had come into my life.

Upon landing, I walked with my fellow passengers across the tarmac, and as soon as I went through the glass door into the building, I rushed to find Mommy and Daddy among the friends and relatives crowding nearby. There they were, smiling and waving in a blur of other people. Hurrying forward in what seemed a race to see who hugged first, we all won as we made it a three person circle of arms.

Mommy was the first to find words.

"Oh, my dear little girl, how we have longed for this moment!"

"Me too!" I managed to say, amid joyous tears and hugs and kisses.

Once all of us jumped into the Ford Fairlane, I caught Daddy's eye as he looked into the driver's mirror and smiled at me in the backseat. He guided that fancy new automobile with perfect ease, quite a contrast to the jerky movements necessary in handling the older cars and trucks he had had before.

Much happy conversation and laughter followed, with Mommy in the front, turning to face me for the entire distance of one hundred miles. Now, entering our driveway, I felt pure joy to see my brother Gene coming out to welcome me. My heart went out to him, because he had worked very hard through his teenage years. Often he had missed school to help Daddy cut pines from the mountains and load them on the old pick-up truck, hauling them to town to sell for the cash necessary to buy household and farm supplies. I hoped that his life had started to become easier now, through Jerry's help.

Mommy and Daddy gave me a tour of the house, showing me their ideas for a remodel. They were proud to point out some modern furniture items, and I sent a silent thanks to Jerry. I could just see how he would be smiling soon as I told him over the phone about our house in Georgia bursting with new chairs, and copper pots and pans shining next to a new refrigerator and stove in the kitchen.

"I really feel most happy about the electric stove," Mommy said. She beamed, showing me its convenient features.

"Of course, the freezer is great too," she said, as she whisked me into a new combination pantry and laundry room, bright white and filled with useful shelving. She opened the freezer doors, so I could see how she and Daddy had already been busy stocking it with vegetables and items that would have been luxurious in my childhood, like frozen orange juice.

After several days of joyous activity with Mommy and Daddy, Colleen and Charles arrived for the weekend. Before the first evening had passed, my ever practical sister was forthright with the question I had dreaded.

"Tell me about this wonderful man who is now a big part of your life?"

I started to talk about Jerry and the many exciting things we had been doing, although I tried to steer clear of any hint of our romantic relationship. Colleen kept making sounds of excitement and expressing pleasure for my life now, but all the while I could tell she was impatient to ask me something more. Listening to my stories about Jerry's friends and the clubs and restaurants we visited, she fastened her eyes on my face, as if she were weighing each of my words and searching for a deeper meaning. Soon enough the question popped out.

"It looks like Jerry is interested in marriage, doesn't it?"

Startled, I just looked at her, unsure what to say. I could tell my Mommy and Daddy were listening closely and anxiously.

Colleen went on, "I know there has not been any intimacy between you two, but I also know that people will be talking about you, unmarried as you are, and we don't want that, do we?"

I felt stunned, the wind taken out of my sails for a moment. My thought flashed back to the scene with the preacher, worried about me reading too many books with Mr. Hagan -- a moment forever etched in my consciousness. As I looked at Colleen, I realized with a pang that no matter how many years would pass, I would always be, in the eyes of my sister, too careless about what people might think. I hoped my parents might be more open-minded, but I couldn't be sure.

All I could be sure of, in that moment, was my love for Jerry. I calmed myself with special memories of the winter and spring, including those glittering hours on the yacht. I could feel sympathy for Colleen, knowing that her life so far had not held such pleasures and joys as mine held now.

Much as I appreciated the summer with Mommy and Daddy, I felt eager to fly back to Jerry, and to pick up my life where I had left it. Whenever the phone rang, I jumped up quickly, hoping it was Jerry, and I wrote him letter after letter, just as he wrote to me.

One day in July, Jerry phoned to tell me he had taken the liberty of renting me an apartment in the Beaux Arts Hotel, in Manhattan, near 43rd Street and Lexington. He said it was nicely furnished, with a spacious bedroom and living room. The kitchen was small, but as Jerry said on the phone, "You'll hardly use the kitchen at all, since I have so many plans for you and sights I want you to see. By the way, today I purchased some nice soft blue pillows, the same shade of blue as your eyes, and I look forward to seeing you relax on them."

After our warm intimate conversation, I looked out the window of our farmhouse. Daddy and Mommy were waiting for me, ready to go to the garden bean patch on the side of the mountain. They had the motor of the little red tractor running. I rushed outside, and Mommy gave me a hug as soon as I joined her. A flatbed trailer was attached to the back of the tractor, and Mommy and I sat together chatting and swinging our feet off the back of the floorboard. Daddy glanced over his shoulder at us occasionally and smiled contentedly as he rounded the curves and went up the mountainside. They were so happy to have me back.

I dreaded saying goodbye in just a few weeks, in spite of my eagerness to see Jerry. The summer had been so much fun: putting on my old work clothes, doing the chores and living exactly as I had in my teenage years. I was especially happy now being at home; since my family's living conditions were better. Because I was now surrounded by so much wealth when I was with Jerry, I often daydreamed about how I'd love to add more luxuries to my parents' household. I realized, however, as we reached the bean patch and I jumped off the flatbed trailer, that I'd never change who my Mommy and Daddy were - just two hard working individuals who always felt most happy when they were busily productive, working on the farm. I picked beans that day in the field until dusk, thinking wistfully about how much fun it would also be in New York, snuggling on those blue pillows with my sweet Prince.

Figure 6: With Jerry at the 21 Club (Comedian Joe E. Lewis is on the right)

15: On to New York

Separating myself from the loving yet clinging arms of Mommy and Daddy at the Atlanta Airport, I had to fight that same old urge grabbing my heart: to stay with them forever, and never, ever leave them. After walking across the tarmac and up the steps to the airplane, I turned and waved one more time to those two people I loved so much.

I had told them I would be staying at the Beaux Arts Hotel in August, while I continued to model, hoping this small fib would be alright. I would indeed be staying in an apartment in that hotel sometimes, but I would not be modeling, and most of my time would be spent with Jerry. I felt grateful that Mommy and Daddy -- unlike Colleen -- refrained from asking me all the questions that might have occurred to them. I wished I could tell my family the whole truth, but I had become used to having to veil my life from them. I encouraged myself by remembering that had I not taken that secret trip to Miami two years earlier, I would not have been privileged to see my deserving Mommy and Daddy enjoying their modernized home and traveling in that new Fairlane instead of the old 1939 Dodge pick-up truck.

A young woman in a Delta uniform greeted me.

"Miss Warren, I am your hostess. I would like to escort you

215

to your seat and take care of any need you might have, to make your flight with us more comfortable."

I smiled, remembering Jerry's promise over the phone the day before. He had told me that his friend Ted, the CEO of Delta, would see that I would be upgraded to VIP status. How much more luxurious this plane ride would be than my first trip out of Atlanta by Greyhound bus, with only a few dollars in my purse! Now I wore a beautiful powder-blue suit that Jerry had bought for me at Joan's salon, and I had no worry about money. Jerry had told me it would be a tight squeeze to get us from the airport to a special party that night, and he had suggested that I make my journey in this particular suit, which he loved to see me wear.

A little over two hours later, the plane began to descend into Idlewild Airport (now JFK). The pain I had experienced at saying goodbye to Mommy and Daddy now vanished, as I felt the electrifying excitement of knowing that as soon as we landed I would be in Jerry's arms. In the following years, my arrival in New York would always hold great happiness, yet this first time would remain the most intense and powerful, because the experience was so new.

Jerry picked me up in that white Cadillac and whisked us to the party at the 21 Club, where we would have dinner with the Sullivans and Bill Paley, president of Columbia Broadcasting Company. Even though my blue suit was a bit wrinkled, I felt I was dressed even fancier than Vivien Leigh had been, when Clark Gable escorted her to the premiere of *Gone with the Wind*.

At the 21 Club, I instantly caught sight of a group of Jerry's friends, who had taken me into their Miami circle with friendliness and even enthusiasm. Ed and Sylvia were chatting with Frank Sinatra, who was with his girlfriend, celebrated dancer Juliet Prowse. As soon as Sylvia saw Jerry and me, she stood, and after giving each of us a hug, she directed Jerry to sit on her left and me beside Jerry.

Smiling broadly she said, "Now Dean, I have placed you between Jerry and Joe Kennedy, because I know how he loves to talk with you."

That brought a smile to the faces of the other guests, who were friends with Joe Kennedy and his son, Senator Jack Kennedy of Massachusetts, and Jack's wife Jackie. Joe Kennedy had become an influential and well-established figure -- a wealthy businessman, a leader of the Democratic Party, an ambassador to England before World War II, and the head of the large and important Irish Catholic Kennedy clan. It was also rumored that he had been a bootlegger during the Prohibition era. At gatherings of Jerry's friends, Joe would often ask to be placed beside me, and he urged me to tell him about my Appalachian childhood. He especially enjoyed my story of sliding in the liquid that escaped from the fermented corn mash at my Daddy's moonshine still.

Our fun conversation ended with Joe Kennedy patting me on the back and remarking, "Dean, you were a little rebel, like me."

Plates were filled with caviar and then grilled fish or steak,

217

covered in delicate sauces, and some desserts came to us flaming with brandy, giving everyone's faces an otherworldly effect. I felt swept up into a world so different from the one I had been enjoying in Georgia with Mommy and Daddy. As I tasted the luscious food at the 21 Club and laughed at people's anecdotes, I found myself thinking of the cornbread and beans my family still liked to eat, sometimes with the addition of fresh river trout or fried chicken, and the blueberry buckle or half-moon pies my Mommy would often serve for dessert, just as Grandma had. I wondered what these rich, well-dressed people would think, if they could see me in my old jeans, picking green beans, feeding my parents' mules, and sitting on the porch with my parents in the evening, as we watched the fireflies, chatting about the crops or telling the familiar family stories.

Looking back, I marvel that I was not nervous or floundering in my conversations with all those sophisticated people. From the start of our relationship, Jerry had encouraged me to feel as comfortable as if I had been born among them. I did feel comfortable, yet I also knew that it had been my hardscrabble childhood in Georgia, in the midst of my loving family, that had shaped me and given me my identity. That night at the 21 Club, as I tasted a slice of angel food cake covered in strawberries, I gave an inner thanks to my parents and my Grandma for their love and care in raising me.

Now the best part of the evening began. Jerry and I excused

ourselves and said goodbye to this circle of friends. Outside the 21 Club, breathing the fresh, expensive air, we waited as the doorman hailed a cab for us. Jerry asked if I would like to come home to the Delmonico with him tonight and go to my own place at the Beaux Arts Hotel one day soon.

"You don't have to ask!" I said, squeezing Jerry's hand.

A few blocks later, the doorman opened the door into the Delmonico and bowed, saying in an Irish accent, "Goodnight, Mr. Brady and Miss Warren."

"Thank you, Mike," said Jerry. "Have a good evening."

I felt flattered that Jerry had already told the staff of the hotel that I would be his guest. In those days, it was not considered acceptable social behavior for an unmarried couple to be alone in a hotel, but somehow Jerry had smoothed the way and made my presence alright.

As we waited in the lobby for the elevator, Jerry whispered in my ear, "Mike handled that goodnight to both of us like a pro, as if me taking a lady into my home was a common occurrence."

"You still don't have a lady!" I tossed my head and smiled mischievously at him.

"And I'll most likely get arrested for incorrect behavior with a minor!"

The mahogany elevator arrived and, along with several other people, we ascended floor by floor, slowly unloading the dignified and proper others. The nimble white-gloved operator of that fancy antique elevator then took us to the penthouse.

Walking on air down the hall to Jerry's door, I stood beside him as he turned the key to his home, my nostrils expanding as his "rich-person" perfume permeated my senses, lighting my eagerness to experience the joy that I knew was once again awaiting me in the bedroom.

My happiness with Jerry that August rippled out to include all of our New York friends. Far from being as "high falutin'" as I might have thought they would be, most of them surprised me by their warm, compassionate nature. Although they had such wealth and education, they were keenly aware of the big difference between the haves and have nots in our country. Jerry especially proved to be energetically indignant about any injustice. This was a bond I quickly realized I had with him. I had always been bothered about the fact that because I was white as I grew up in the South, I had special privileges. Ellijay's population was completely white, and even though my family and our neighbors had been poor in my childhood, we had felt protected by the color of our skin.

One morning, as Jerry and I lingered over breakfast, I told him the story of a trip I had taken with my Daddy when I was about seven years old. We had driven in our old Model A pick-up truck through an adjoining county. On our way home, in the growing dusk, Daddy stopped at a mountain spring beside the road. He lit the lantern, and then we spread our supper of saltine crackers and tinned sardines on the running board. As we ate, we enjoyed relaxing and hearing the whippoorwills and crickets. Daddy and I considered our supper to be a delicacy (although I don't think we had ever heard the word "delicacy"). After we ate, we gulped down water from a gourd, which we used both for drinking and for filling the radiator so the truck wouldn't overheat.

That was when Daddy lifted our lighted lantern and showed me a sign beside the road. He read aloud, "'*Negro, don't let the sun set on you in White County.*'"

I looked at Daddy, hoping he would explain. He said soberly, "You know, Odean, we could get killed being here now at dark if our skin color was black."

Later that night, lying in bed beside Grandma, I began to cry, thinking about how sad it was that if my Daddy was black he could be dead.

My Grandma hugged me close and whispered in my ear, "Let's don't wake Mommy and Daddy hearing you cry, because they have a hard day of work tomorrow."

Jerry responded to that story as he always did, with a tender hug. He held me close, as if he wished he could go back in time and comfort me, just as my Grandma had.

Soon after, I told Ed and Sylvia about that road sign in Georgia. Ed spoke right up.

"Dean, thank you for that story. But prejudice is not only an issue in the South . . ."

221

Sylvia quickly followed out Ed's thought. Leaning toward me, she said, "There is still much prejudice here. Jerry, tell Dean about the afternoon Lena Horne came to the Delmonico."

Jerry shared the story of one afternoon a year or so earlier, when Lena Horne and her manager had an appointment to see Ed in his office upstairs at the Delmonico. The doorman suggested that the lady should go around to the delivery service door, since she was African American.

Miss Horne's manager took the house phone and called Ed. Upon hearing about Miss Horne's reception by the doorman, Ed became livid and rushed to take the elevator down. Jerry, who was visiting, went down to the lobby with him.

After telling this story, Jerry turned to Ed and said, "Ed, I've never seen you so angry as when you blasted the hotel manager. You told him, 'Miss Horne is my guest and she will go up in the front elevator with me.'"

In the next few years, I went to several of Lena Horne's performances, and I so enjoyed hearing her and being in her presence. A couple of times I was privileged to sit beside her at the Sullivans' table, which was always ringside.

Many times during these later years, I have wished Ed, Sylvia and Jerry could have had the same privilege I have had of seeing an African American become our president.

That summer, my own world quickly grew larger than I could ever have imagined. Within a day or two of my arrival, I opened the door to my new apartment at the Beaux Arts Hotel, looking out on the United Nations. I was grateful to have this special foothold in New York, in addition to Jerry's home at the Delmonico. Most of the tenants in the Beaux Arts were young and vibrant workers at the UN or foreign students who were interested in world politics. It was also a favorite of airline stewardesses and pilots, in between national and international flights.

One day in mid-August, my kitchen phone rang. It was Jerry downstairs in the lobby.

"Yes, I am ready and relaxing on my special blue pillows!" I said. "I'll be downstairs in a few minutes."

We would be meeting Ed and Sylvia again for dinner at the Pavillon, a highly exclusive French restaurant at 57th and Park Avenue, where many celebrities and political figures gathered. I did a pivot turn, admiring the image of myself in the floor length mirror, approving my bright blue dress, which matched the blue pillows. Jerry had chosen this dress, as he chose most of my clothes at first. I smiled, remembering how he had shopped for me in Joan Gaines' Salon in Miami. He had selected more elaborate styles then, but now he was happier seeing me in clothes that were more youthful and simple. He liked my hairdo in a bun for evenings, but a ponytail was still his favorite when we were on more casual dates.

When we entered the Pavillon, Henri Soule, the owner, greeted us and brought us over to Sylvia and Ed, who were sitting in their favorite booth. I always found it a bit surprising that in the major restaurants and nightclubs, celebrities like the Sullivans had special booths or tables, and if they called for a reservation, that spot would be waiting for them.

Soon after the waiter brought our drinks, Ed started the conversation in the way he usually did -- by encouraging Jerry to tell of some experience or adventure. Even though Ed and Sylvia knew practically all of Jerry's stories, Ed especially enjoyed seeing me hear them for the first time.

"Jerry, have you told Dean yet about the time Al Capone tried to give you a gift?"

Jerry laughed and shook his head. "Not yet."

"Well, then," Ed said, grinning, "how about telling it now?"

As always, Jerry spoke in a compact and exciting way, captivating his listeners. Now as I repeat the story in my words, I miss Jerry's animated smile and warm pleasing voice.

Here is how the story went:

It was an early morning in the paddock of the Kentucky Derby, the first year Jerry was employed at The American Totalisator Company. Mrs. Vanderbilt, the formidable heiress of the Vanderbilt fortune, was visiting. Jerry had become friends with her and her son Alfred during Jerry's college years, when he had helped her with the accounts for her racing stables. She had a thoroughbred

224

horse that had not won any races, and she was hopeful that this time her horse would prove a winner.

Jerry greeted Mrs. Vanderbilt as she stood beside her horse in the paddock, caressing its muzzle. A bunch of other hopeful horse owners waited just outside the paddock fence, as the horses were brought out for their early morning exercise run.

Jerry had to be very careful about not giving out any tips about the horses, since he worked for the company that created and ran the tote boards ("tote" was short for Totalisator), large electronic machines that showed the odds on each horse.

One of the horse owners -- a friend of Jerry's -- asked him breezily, "I know you don't give out tips about which horse you think might win, but I'm just curious to know -- which one do you think looks ready to take the lead and win in this race?"

Jerry was preoccupied, and just responded to this question honestly, without thinking about what he should or shouldn't say, or who might be listening.

"Of course no one knows which one will be the winner," he said, "but I like the energy and speed of a particular horse, and it happens to be the Vanderbilt horse."

Unknown to Jerry, Al Capone, the top gangster of that generation, overheard the comment Jerry made. He rushed down and placed a huge amount of money on Mrs. Vanderbilt's horse. Amazingly, Jerry was right, and her horse won for the first time.

After the race, Jerry escorted Mrs. Vanderbilt back down to the paddock, because she wanted to pet her horse for his great win. As they approached the paddock, Al Capone flagged Jerry down. He said quietly, "Mr. Brady, thank you for that tip you gave your friend. I rushed down to the tote machines and placed a pile of money on that horse."

Jerry was flabbergasted, and at first couldn't even remember what the heck Mr. Capone was talking about. As soon as he remembered chatting with his friend, Jerry felt flooded with embarrassment. Mrs. Vanderbilt was a few steps ahead of them, and he hoped she hadn't been listening to this conversation.

The worst was yet to come, however. When Al Capone reached to shake Jerry's hand, Jerry realized that Capone's hand was stuffed with a roll of money. Jerry kept trying to push the wad of bills back into his hand before Mrs. Vanderbilt saw what was happening. He managed to get the bills back into Capone's hand, thank heavens, and breathed a great sigh of relief.

Once Jerry came back to Mrs. Vanderbilt's side, though, she raised her eyebrows and then whispered into his ear, "Isn't that the terrible gangster, Al Capone?"

Jerry said simply, "Yes."

The next few days of her stay, Jerry waited to hear the news that he was fired, because she might tell his company that he gave out tips and fixed races. As it turned out, whether or not Mrs.

Vanderbilt knew about Al Capone's gratitude for the tip, she never mentioned it, and Jerry was able to keep his successful career.

Jerry, however, always said he learned a lesson that day, which would serve him well. He decided to resist the urge to give his opinion on a horse's chances to Al Capone or anyone else. It was important to Jerry to have integrity and a sense of honor. Luckily, he had a wonderful sense of humor, too, and a gift for storytelling that reminded me of my family in Georgia.

Figure 7: Ed Sullivan (left) with Mr. and Mrs. David Marx of the toy empire. Sylvia Sullivan, next to Jerry.

16: Love Confirmed

Over the course of that warm summer in the city, Jerry and I expressed how much we loved each other, and how wholeheartedly we wanted to be with each other from now on. Once August came to an end, Jerry and I gladly agreed that I would stay in New York until both of us went to Miami together.

Soon I landed a job as a model at the Seymour Fox Fur Salon. It was a great relief to know that what I had told my parents about my modeling job in New York City was now true. This salon was different from the bustling, lively Gaines salon in Miami Beach. At Seymour Fox, furs were shown by appointment only. Madame Colette, the French salon manager, would drape and carefully arrange the furs on me so they would show to their best advantage. In my ingénue persona, I would then, under Colette's watchful eye, glide around the champagne-drinking customers, while Seymour charmed them into a relaxed and ready-to-buy state. I often thought about the differences between me and these ultra-heavily jeweled female customers, who epitomized the height of fashion. In my earlier days, I might have envied them. Now, however, I just smiled to myself. I was crazy in love with Jerry, and I knew, right down to my little toes, how much more important love and affection were than the most fabulous and ostentatious wealth.

On one particular morning, after having finished my hours modeling, I walked to the ladies' lounge to change into the walking shoes Jerry had bought for me. I was experiencing a totally new approach to foot care as I enjoyed my daily strolls to and from the Beaux Arts Hotel. As soon as I stepped foot in the lounge, I needed to adjust to the firmness of the tiled floor, after having spent hours walking on the thick carpet of the salon. The change to firmness was pleasing and I instantly felt more grounded.

I held the door open for Madame Colette, who was coming into the lounge just behind me. She had a little smile on her face as I said hello to her.

In her lilting voice with the French accent, she said, "Oh, my dear, I love your Southern accent! It's so . . . refreshing!" She gave me a brief hug, and added, "To use your Southern slang, 'it cracks me up' each time I think of your interview here!"

I tried to smile, remembering how standoffish she had seemed during my interview. I couldn't help being a little suspicious of her lavishly friendly attitude now. I sat on a banquette and bent over to start putting on my sturdy shoes.

"I was very nervous then," I said.

Madame Colette started brushing her hair, in front of one of the huge mirrors edged in a gilt frame.

Catching my eye in the mirror, she said, "I'm not referring to your nervousness. In fact, I thought you were quite poised. Though

I was amused at what Mr. Fox and Mr. Brady said just after you left."

I paused in my shoelace tying, and looked up at Madame Colette as I waited to hear more. I felt startled to realize that Jerry and Mr. Fox had spoken about me in front of Madame Colette.

She went on, as she powdered her face and applied lipstick. She was clearly relishing her story.

"Mr. Fox was saying you should develop a sophisticated look, but Mr. Brady jumped up and disagreed." Madame Colette turned around from the mirror, and waved her hands in the air a bit, as she imitated Jerry. "He said, 'Oh no, don't have her be like that! It's not Deany!'" She laughed.

I ignored her tone as I said excitedly, "He called me Deany!? That sounds so endearing! I wish I could have heard him say that."

Madame smiled a little. "You two are obviously in love," she said drily. "That in itself is refreshing." She crossed her arms and leaned against the vanity counter. "But to get back to my story. Mr. Fox looked surprised, and then he said, 'Well, we will have Deany display an innocent girl's excitement at having a millionaire friend who is purchasing her furs!'"

Madame Colette laughed, as she looked at me curiously, to see my reaction. I blushed and couldn't think what to say, ducking my head down as I finished tying my shoes. I caught the innuendo in her story, calling into question my innocence and hinting that I was after Jerry's money.

"I am pleased to add," Madame Colette said, "most of our customers seem to approve of the difference between you and the more sophisticated models and I certainly enjoy seeing Mr. Brady so happy. Mr. Fox and his aunt Joan Gaines have been dear friends of Jerry's for years."

I couldn't help noticing her emphasis on "sophisticated," and her suggestion that I did not have this important quality. I also felt the way in which she seemed to draw a boundary between Jerry's "dear friends" and me. I felt surprised that she had slipped out of her formality to call Jerry by his first name, and I couldn't help wondering if she too was a "dear friend" of Jerry's.

With my shoes on, I stood up to go. Before I left, though, I looked straight at Madame Colette, my head held high. I could feel some of my family's pride and stubbornness rising up in me.

"I am aware," I said, "that many beautiful models pound the pavement for years and never get such a choice modeling job as I am now enjoying. I want you to know, I do work hard at it and I'm grateful for the chance."

I stopped short of saying that I felt guilty about my good fortune -- I did not want to confess this to her -- but Madame Colette seemed to understand this without my having to say it. For a brief moment, in fact, she seemed to lay down her weapons.

Touching my arm, she said softly, "Of course. And you mustn't feel guilty, just enjoy the privilege. Looking into your eyes, I sense life has not been easy for you up to this point."

I moved toward her and we met in a quick embrace.

"Thank you," I said, and then I walked as gracefully as I could out of the lounge. I tried to shake off the discomfort of our conversation and to keep hold of the sense of dignity and self-worth I knew my family had raised me to have.

My usual enjoyable walk home that evening was more pensive than on other days. I had a gut feeling that Madame Colette was not telling me all she knew about Jerry. Well, I thought, whatever may have happened between Jerry and this woman, he is in love with me, and I am head over heels in love with him. Nothing and no one can change that extraordinary fact. Walking home, I let myself feel again the bountiful sense of my new life. I couldn't wait to see Jerry again, and I decided to ask him to call me Deany from now on.

After that encounter with Madame Colette, I tried to have confidence in my relationship with Jerry. I continued to have moments of doubt, however. Could Jerry really continue to love me? He and his friends were so affluent. They moved in the world with trust and self-confidence. I was young and had only a high school education -- wouldn't Jerry start to become bored? Jerry showed no hints of such a change of heart, yet I couldn't help worrying about what other people might be thinking, and what Jerry might one day think himself.

My doubts about Jerry's abiding love for me were soothed, however, after a certain conversation with Jerry, Sylvia and Ed.

On that particular evening I was having a Friday night dinner with Jerry, Ed and Sylvia at the Pavillon. I remember the day being a Friday because Sylvia, in a whisper, had shared an amusing observation about Ed and Jerry's eating habits.

"Now, Deany, you will learn that even though their religion is not an urgent force in their lives today, they still hold to the strict rule of their childhood Catholic background of eating fish on Fridays."

When the waiter brought the menu, Sylvia ordered steak. I felt a bit nervous and rather than read the menu I made it easy for myself by just ordering the same as she did.

When Jerry and Ed looked at the menu, they did order fish. Since she and I were sitting on the cushioned side of the booth and they were seated in chairs facing us, it was easy for her to touch and lightly squeeze my hand under the table, and we shared a fleeting smile.

After the waiter brought our drinks, we sat in a very relaxed mood and I surprised myself by starting the conversation. I had begun to feel less shy, especially around Sylvia and Ed.

"I am just so enamored with the Delmonico Hotel," I said. "I can well imagine it's had an interesting history."

Smiling, Ed said, "Yes, and Jerry is responsible for our personal history at the famous Delmonico. Jerry, why don't you tell Deany how we came to live in the Delmonico?"

Jerry just smiled, and waved his hand.

Ed continued, "Jerry was horrified that we were raising our Betty at the Astor Hotel! He thought it was much too threadbare for an up-and-coming entertainer and his family, especially once Betty became a teenager."

Jerry shook his head, laughing. I knew Ed and Sylvia's apartment now was a beautiful three-bedroom suite on the eleventh floor of the Delmonico. Their daughter had grown up in a comfortable space, with maids and room service. She was about my age -- a fact that had come up sometimes in conversation with the Sullivans.

"Well, then, I am 100% responsible for your move to the Delmonico!" said Jerry, throwing up his hands.

I loved this story, because it brought out Jerry's natural honesty and care for others. I felt as if a light bulb turned on in my brain, just like in those Disney cartoons, and brightened up my world. I saw with fresh clarity that Jerry was someone his friends could count on to say what he felt. In addition, he was a person who cared very much about the safety and happiness of younger people, like Betty Sullivan. In taking the liberty of advising close friends as to the importance of changing their home so as to protect their teenage daughter, he showed a concern that reminded me of his concern for me. Big-hearted, open, and down to earth, Jerry Brady was someone to have and to hold, and I decided I had been a silly goose to doubt it, as my Grandma might have said.

Ed Sullivan: The Side You Don't See on Television

22

The Sullivan's best friends are their old friends, most of whom go back to the early Broadway columning days. The Marxes of the top echelon; the Jerry Bradys of racketick wealth; Rose Shirley, widow of the real estate tycoon who gave his name to Shirley, L. I. A number of close friends are in show business, but are primarily Hollywood-based: the Bob Hopes, the Jack Benny's. The Sullivans don't swing with an actor-dominated crowd.

The closest Sullivan friends at Friar's Club dinner naming him man of the year. With Ed, left, are Mrs. Walter T. Shirley, Sylvia Sullivan, Carmine Seaside (who has been his secretary of 33 years), Mr. and Mrs. Jerry Brady.

"We don't go to the theater often, we never go to cocktail parties, and seldom to formal dinners. When we do, it's usually spur of the moment. Ed hates to have a tied-down feeling, hates to feel that he has to be at a certain place at a certain time," says Sylvia. He has enough of this in his work."

Figure 8: Part of an article from the World Journal Tribune April 1967

237

Figure 9: L to R: Ed, Walter Shirley's wife (Aunt Rose to Jeriann), Sylvia, Ed's assistant Carmine Santullo

17: First the Baby Carriage, Then the Marriage

Five years into our relationship, Jerry and I found it necessary to stop and consider seriously an unplanned event that had developed: I had become pregnant. Previously, we had casually discussed the possibility of marriage, but from opposite standpoints. Jerry felt he was much too old for me and I should consider meeting someone my own age. Each time he said this, I refused to listen, and so the result would be -- subject dropped and another cozy period of lovemaking would erase all thought of change.

One summer morning in 1961, a few weeks after I had missed my period, I hailed a taxicab and visited a doctor friend on my own, without telling Jerry. While I waited for the test results, I was quite casual, but when our friend Dr. Murphy came into his office, the smiling face of this man who had four children made me wish Jerry was by my side. I realized this was a once in a lifetime experience that we could have shared. The "odd couple," as our friends referred to us, were indeed going to have a baby.

Walking back home from Dr. Murphy's office, I felt so grateful to be having this baby with someone I loved with all my heart. So far from feeling the shock and distress of my first pregnancy, which had come out of a mistaken and impersonal encounter, I was already beginning to cherish this baby.

Thinking back, I realized that I might have conceived this new life on a poignant day earlier that summer, when Jerry had discovered that his brother Bill had died. After Fran called him with the sad news, Jerry felt heartbroken. This was the first time I had ever seen him truly cry. Was there a connection between a death and a new birth?

At our building, Mike the doorman opened the door for me with his combined half bow and friendly nod of the head.

Offering me the note in his hand, he said, "Mr. Brady telephoned me and left this message."

The message read, "Deany, I have a meeting at my office. Sylvia and Ed will be picking you up at about 7:00 and I will meet you at the Copa about 7:30."

Yes, of course! I realized that tonight was the night for Frank Sinatra's annual opening at Lou Walters' Copacabana. I had been so caught up in my exciting news, this had slipped my mind. Dressing for the club that afternoon, I wondered how all our friends would respond to this news of a baby coming. They often felt Jerry and I were full of surprises, but this would be a big one!

I kept remembering an evening a few years earlier -- which had also been Frank Sinatra's opening at the Copa -- when Phil Silvers first dubbed us "The Odd Couple." Barbara Walters had been at her father's club, table hopping among guests. Jerry and I had arrived a bit late, so the long mahogany celebrity table was nearly filled, but Sylvia had our name cards marking the place settings beside her. Barbara was momentarily sitting at Jerry's place as she talked with Sylvia.

Phil Silvers rose to announce, "Here comes the Odd Couple!"

Barbara asked Jerry, "Why the Odd Couple?"

Jerry told her, "Deany and I are considered the 'Odd Couple' because we do everything differently than most people."

I loved Jerry's way of putting that. It was true: Jerry and I both had an independent streak. We enjoyed going about things in our own way, sharing a sense of youthful enthusiasm as we plunged into our life together, come what may. One of our greatest pleasures was simply being together. In each other, we felt we had the best riches, and we loved our fun but simple life in New York. Most of our friends lived close to us, within the radius of about ten blocks on Park Avenue or adjacent to it, and some of our closest friends lived in the Pierre Hotel, The Plaza, or the Sherry Netherland, overlooking the elegant southwest corner of Central Park. Jerry and I liked to walk hand and hand together, as we strolled in this beautiful neighborhood. We often walked to dinner at the 21 Club and Toots Shor's. Another favorite was the Waldorf Astoria, which had excellent food, and a gifted pianist, Bobby Short, who would play as we dined. On most evenings the wives walked home separately from their husbands, enjoying the windows displaying jewelry, and making plans to purchase items the following day during luncheon

241

get-togethers. Both Jerry and I, however, thought leisurely and expensive lunches, and constant shopping for luxuries, were a waste of time. Our lack of interest in showy things or extravagance became a source of good-natured amusement among our friends. Now with a baby coming, while most of our friends were enjoying grandchildren, we would enjoy being even more odd!

The morning after my appointment with Dr. Murphy, as Jerry and I had our usual late breakfast in the cozy corner of our kitchen, I looked at him and smiled.

"Jerry, dear, I have news from Dr. Murphy."

"Dr. Murphy?" Jerry looked surprised and a little worried. He held his coffee mug in the air.

I smiled even more broadly and put my hand on his. "Yes! We're going to have a baby."

Jerry's eyes flashed twice their normal size. Looking stricken, he set his mug on the table with a resounding thud. This marked the first time I had ever seen him registering helplessness.

He gazed at me with wonder and anxiety.

"But, Deany, I don't know how to have a baby!"

Then, typical of Jerry, thinking of the other person in every situation he encountered, he jumped from his chair to stand by mine. I stood up and we embraced.

"Deany, I'm sure this is not the storybook reaction a young pregnant mother would like! I'm kind of in shock."

"Oh, don't worry," I said. "I'm pretty shocked myself. Let's go sit on the couch and talk about this."

"Not too close, though," he said with a touch of mischief.

"That doesn't matter now, Mr. Brady!"

We laughed together and that lightened our worries. About midway into our conversation on the couch, Jerry brightened and began to seem more himself.

"It must be a little girl like you!"

"What about a little boy like you, named Jerry, of course."

"Or a little girl named Geraldean?"

"NO, NO, not Geraldean!" we chimed together.

"How about if it's a girl," I said, "she could be 'Jeri,' to honor you, and 'Ann' to honor your sister-in-law Anne? 'Jeriann'?"

Jerry hugged me. "Well, now, it looks like 'Jeriann' has ended our argument of whether we should marry! Next week, let's elope! We can go to Norwalk and see my friend, Judge Nancy Germano."

"Next Tuesday is my birthday."

"Then that is a good day to marry!"

Jerry reached for my telephone and made an appointment for the following Tuesday, August 15th, at 1:00.

We spent the next several days, at times, like a couple of giggly teenagers, and on my birthday, we took the train up to Norwalk and arrived in Judge Germano's office. Her secretary informed us that we must have blood tests before getting married.

She said, "Oh, Jerry, I'm so sorry. I just thought you knew that blood tests are required now before a marriage can take place."

We returned to Judge Germano's office the following Monday with blood test results in hand. So August 21st would forever be our wedding anniversary.

Each year now, on the night of August 21, I celebrate alone that momentous day of my life by remembering a scene in our bedroom on my wedding night. Obviously, I'm not talking about a virgin bridal scene, because we had made love for a few years on that bed in his

penthouse of the Delmonico! This vital memory, instead, is about an experience I had on my own, once Jerry was sound asleep, and I moved in the darkness to a window overlooking Park Avenue. As I knelt near the window sill, I looked first to the left, up Park Avenue, and then to the right, down Park Avenue. Then I let my glance fall to the street level and, observing the height of the Delmonico Hotel, I realized that I was now higher than the mountain I had seen the sun climb up each morning of my childhood.

I whispered to myself, "I'm higher than Yonder Mountain!"

Soon after, I crawled back into bed, beside Jerry's warm peaceful body. Before falling back to sleep, though, I daydreamed again that perpetual dream: how someday I would write a book and its title would be *Higher Than Yonder Mountain.*

Here, after many, many years of living, is that book.

It was a few weeks after our discovery of my pregnancy before Jerry and I began seeing friends again. Both of us needed time to adjust and feel comfortable with this major change in our lives, and in any case, most of our closest friends were out of the city during the hot, humid days of late summer. The Sullivans were in Europe and others were relaxing in their summer homes in the Catskills or along the Atlantic Coast as far north as Maine.

Once the Sullivans had come home, Sylvia telephoned and invited us to join them at Toots Shor's restaurant for dinner. Jerry talked awhile to Sylvia on the phone, and then she asked to speak to me. We had a fun chat as always, and I thanked her for the lovely bag she had sent me from Paris. Listening to our conversation, Jerry became aware of the fact that he had not thanked her for the ties she had sent him, and he motioned he would like the phone back so he could thank her too.

After Jerry and Sylvia talked a bit more, Jerry looked at me and repeated her words.

"So Danny Arnstein and Eddie Weisel and his wife Alice will be joining us?" Jerry gave me a quizzical look as if to ask, "Is that alright with you?"

I responded with a nod, although I would rather it had been just the four of us when we shared news of the baby. But no way was I going to refuse to spend an evening with all of these good friends.

Entering Toots and his wife Baby Shor's restaurant was always a thrill. Celebrities and other friends came by Ed and Sylvia's special table, and tourists, as usual, asked for Ed's autograph. He was so nice as he willingly stopped eating to smile and chat a bit, whether he knew the people or not.

I was nervous on this night because I knew attention would be focused on Jerry and me once he announced our good news. When the cheerful dinner was finished, and the desserts were about to be served, I could tell Jerry was getting ready to tell our friends about our baby coming. As it turned out, the conversation at the table turned instead to Eddie Weisel's unique and passionate hobby of "reading" craniums. I was already familiar with his hobby, because he had massaged and examined my cranium several times as we sat on the beach near Danny's home in Miami Beach. Each time Eddie had searched for information, as he studied my head, he had come up with some flattering descriptions, indicating that there was a highly creative mind inside, whereas by comparison, Jerry's cranium was smooth, indicating more matter-of-factness.

As soon as Eddie paused in his discussion of craniums (a subject that baffled his friends, because it was so opposite to his brilliant work as a lawyer), Jerry leaned over and clinked on his water glass.

With his arm around my shoulders, he said with a smile, "Deany and I have a life-changing announcement."

An expectant silence hovered over our table. Then Ed raised his wine glass, grinning and flushing with delight. "It's about time you got engaged!"

"For once you're wrong, Ed," said Jerry. "This time we're announcing the arrival of our baby!"

"WHAT!" was the leading surprised comment, as our table burst into a chorus of congratulations and good wishes.

Raising her glass, Sylvia said, "I am speechless, yet filled to overflowing with joy, hearing this great news."

She turned to hug Jerry as she cried and laughed at the same time. The candlelight from the table sparkled in Jerry's eyes, brimming with happiness.

Then Sylvia leaned across Jerry to give me a huge hug, softly saying, "I have been longing to see this day," as those strong hands of hers squeezed mine with deep affection.

Ed came over to hug me, followed by the other guests at our table. The whole restaurant seemed to be enjoying our friends' outburst of joy and surprise. Baby and Toots Shor ordered champagne for our table and came over to join us. Everyone settled back to await the champagne, and Jerry again started the conversation by raising his sherry glass.

"Of course, Ed is actually right about the second half of our news, and we might as well tell you now. Deany and I did tie the knot, a few weeks ago, up in Connecticut!"

Our table erupted again in a flurry of congratulations. Once the champagne arrived, Jerry offered a toast to his new bride, and our coming baby.

Then he turned to Eddie Weisel with a smile, saying, "Now let's get back to the subject of craniums, with the hope that our baby will inherit a rough, knotty cranium like Deany's instead of my boring smooth one."

Raising his glass, Eddie offered a toast. "To the young marrieds, who have found a subject far more interesting than craniums."

Henri Soule and the Sullivans soon held a festive dinner in our honor at Henri's Pavillon. After this wonderful celebration, Jerry and I felt ready to come back to our quiet life together. For the following months, we enjoyed our time on our own, and went out only rarely with friends. Our disappearing from the social scene in which we had been so immersed caused some friends distress, especially Sylvia, as I realized one day when she and I spoke on the phone.

"Jerry is no longer seeing the forest for the trees!" she said.

I felt startled. I couldn't think what to say, and I tried to let Sylvia's words flow like water off a duck's back.

When I told Jerry about this conversation, he burst out, "Now, what the heck does *that* mean?"

The way Jerry put this made me laugh, and soon we switched to other subjects, including all we had to get done before the thoroughbred racing season was well underway at Tropical Park in Miami.

Jerry brought out his usual list of "to be done before Christmas," so that we could be ready to get to our winter home in Miami by January 1st. This time, his list included moving to a larger apartment at 225 East 57th Street, seeing the Macy's Christmas Parade, and finding a reputable obstetrician and pediatrician in Miami, so that I could give birth there.

We did accomplish most of those things, but the one question remaining was where I would continue my pregnancy and have the baby. Jerry insisted that he'd love to be near me through my whole pregnancy and see the baby as soon as she was born. I pleaded with Jerry to let me go straight to Georgia, however, instead of to Miami. Jerry couldn't accept one of my reasons: that I would be getting "fatter and fatter." "You will be getting more and more beautiful," he said. Yet he felt somewhat more persuaded by my additional wish to be home with my Mommy and Daddy, and near Colleen, who was a nurse at the hospital where I could give birth.

So we compromised that I would be in Miami with Jerry until the last few weeks of my pregnancy. The baby was due in early March.

Miami Beach felt like home, and yet it felt new too, now that I was pregnant. I enjoyed the warmth and the bright sun over the ocean even more than usual, after New York's cold winter. With Frank Sinatra's opening coming up in mid-January, I knew I would need some pretty maternity outfit, so Jerry and I went shopping at Jordan Marsh. Before we entered the store, I said to Jerry, "Let's stop by that park bench on Biscayne where you used to pick me up at 5:00."

"Funny how I was just starting to say we should do that. I must be getting as sentimental as you!"

On the evening of Frank's opening, I wore a royal blue maternity jumper that hung loosely over a white ruffled silk blouse. Seated around our regular ringside table were Ed and Sylvia, Tony Bennett, Dean Martin, and about a dozen of our other friends. The evening was long and very festive, and in the late hours, everyone was getting more and more mellow. Frank, with his mike in hand, walked near our end of the table and, leaning over us, started to sing the well-known song "Love and Marriage."

Jerry and I smiled as we anticipated this song: "Love and marriage, love and marriage, / Go together like a horse and carriage, / . . . You can't have one without the other."

Quickly we realized, though, that Frank had mischievously changed the lyrics.

"Love and Marriage, love and marriage / First you have to have the Baby carriage / Then you have the Marriage."

Jerry whispered in my ear, "Oh, Mr. Pure."

That spring Jerry gave his blessing as I returned to Georgia to have our baby closer to my family. I hugged him close in the airport, and he patted my belly.

"Goodbye, baby," he whispered to our baby inside. "I'll see you when you come out into this world."

He watched me walk onto the plane, and I felt sure he waited until the plane was high in the sky before he drove back to the city.

Figure 10: Taken by Bloomingdale's Photography in New York

Figure 11: In Ed and Sylvia's Home

Figure 12: Ed Sullivan with my Mommy, my Daddy, my brother Gene, and his wife Edith

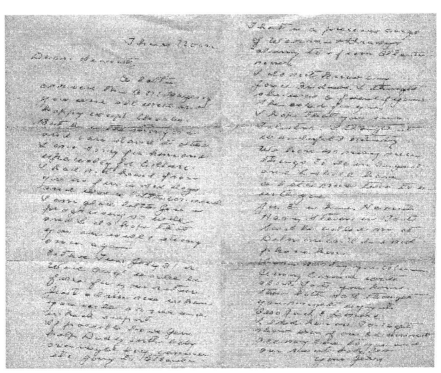

Figure 13: Letter from Jerry

18: The Glorious Years: Jeriann from Baby to Six

It was good to be home, helping to prepare healthy, simple meals with Mommy, and sharing them with Mommy and Daddy, as we talked about neighbors and plans for the farm. They were eager for stories about my life with Jerry in New York and Miami Beach, especially now that I had become an honest, married woman! This was a special time of peace and contentment with my family, before the birth.

As the baby's due date approached, I went to stay with Colleen and Charles in Rome, Georgia. Once my labor started, Colleen helped constantly, with calmness and expert care, both at her house and in the hospital. The labor was long and painful, however, and the doctor gave me so much pain medicine for the birth that it took both the baby and me four days to recover. Jeriann had to remain in an incubator in the neonatal unit until the fifth day, when I could finally hold her in my arms.

Luckily, I did get news of Jeriann's progress, since Mommy and Daddy passed my room each morning, without even a glance inside, on their urgent mission to see her. Then they would be smiling as they came back to my room to hug me and place huge bunches of March flowers, which were flourishing in their flower

257

garden. Each hour, they would rush out to see the baby, and come back to my side, filled with news of her sweet perfections.

Jerry sent big bunches of flowers, and telegrams filled with expressions of love and joy. I knew he couldn't wait to see us both.

I felt a heart full of gratitude to Colleen, who took care of Jeriann and me during and after the birthing process in the hospital. Jerry, of course, sent her a generous check. She thanked him profusely, excited to renovate her home and buy new appliances. I felt glad that Jerry could help Colleen in this way, since she had helped me so much with the baby.

At home in Ellijay again, as I got my strength back, I delighted daily in Mommy and Daddy's happiness as grandparents. They became younger before my eyes, as they held baby Jeriann and sang all the songs I remembered from my own early childhood. Mommy's graceful handling of baby Jeriann was a great learning experience. It enabled me to hone my talents in parenting, since I was awkward in that area. I expected to find Jerry even more ill at ease, because in all his bachelor years he had not been around babies. I felt it necessary to absorb as much practical knowledge as possible from my parents, about diapering, feeding, and soothing my infant. Little did I know that Jerry would prove to be a natural at baby care, and would most definitely put me to shame with his wonderful instincts.

Those two months gave me time not only to regain my health, but to contemplate my life in a fresh way. Often I sat on the bank beside the creek to daydream again, as I had done in my girlhood. I was not now dreaming of a better life for my family and me -- that dream had come true for all of us, soon after I met Jerry. Now my wish was to get back to Jerry and feel the joy of sharing care of our baby Jeriann.

Much as I felt thankful for Colleen, she could still get under my skin. On one of her visits to Ellijay, she and I were reminiscing about our childhood together.

"Remember when you had to bring me back from the Andy Spring?" I said. "You'd have to stop your own chores and walk all that way to fetch me."

Colleen smiled a little mischievously. "Yes, I can see you now, so innocently walking across the valley and up the mountain. You would be nonchalantly swinging a bucket in your hand. For a time, we couldn't guess you would have sneaked a book inside the empty bucket, so you could sit on the root of a big oak tree and read. Often you'd forget to bring the drinking water back!"

She and I laughed, but then came the zinger.

"I'm so glad you're going back home to Jerry," she said. "I'm sure your friends are already talking about this strange marriage you and Jerry have."

I just shrugged and laughed, making a joke of it, although I felt upset. I gathered that Colleen meant our marriage was strange because Jerry was so much older than I was.

"Well, we've grown used to being the Odd Couple," I said. "We like it that way."

Waving to Colleen and Charles as they left our driveway, however, my irritation with Colleen melted, and I felt a renewed surge of love for her. She couldn't help caring so much about other people's opinions. In my heart, I wished Colleen could have had a taste of the happiness my life with my silver-haired Prince had brought me.

Jerry was waiting at the gate with a huge smile when I arrived with Jeriann. He rushed toward us, but our longed-for meeting was a little more awkward than the one I had been imagining. As I approached, I wanted to give him a huge hug as I had done so many times before, when he had met me at Idlewild. However, at that moment, if I reached to hug him, I would drop the baby! He also seemed slightly confused about which of us to hug first, so we managed a delicate three-way hug, even before he could see Jeriann's face, in her little pink blanket. To my surprise, I felt his body trembling as he reached for Jeriann, and by the time he had lifted her to snuggle her tiny face against his, a stream of tears was flowing down his face. He was not given to easy tears, as I was, and I realized this was only the second time I had seen him cry.

After we had recovered from all the newness, excitement and awkwardness, we managed to do a great job of tucking baby into the car's fancy carriage bed. She opened those big brown eyes and stared straight into Jerry's eyes, sending him back into an ecstatic emotional loop again.

As Jerry drove carefully home, he told me everyone was wanting to come see me and the baby.

"Sylvia wanted to drive me to the airport and help you get settled, but I didn't accept her offer, since I wanted to be just with you when I finally met our baby."

I felt a twinge of guilt. Maybe getting fat in glamorous Miami wouldn't have been so bad after all, since not seeing his baby at her birth, and for her first two months, had been harder on him than I had realized. He had our baby close now, though, and I looked ahead with happiness to sharing her with her proud dad. Jerry clearly felt the same urge to make up for lost time. Once we were home, he wouldn't let any friends come over for the first few days.

Later, during our first heavenly month back home, our friends often came to visit, especially in the early evenings, on their way to restaurants and clubs. After all their oohing and ahhhing and cooing as they held her, most everyone got a laugh from realizing that Jerry was still in his pajamas at that evening hour. Jerry had no time to get dressed, as he spent every waking moment with Jeriann.

Once Ed remarked, "Jerry, this is really cool. I haven't seen you in pajamas since we were boys, and I'd come by your house to shoot hoops in your backyard and sometimes you'd still be in your jammies."

During that first summer with baby Jeriann blessing our lives, our bliss blossomed to its fullest. For me especially, it was a time when I felt the need to consider more seriously the source from which all this bounty flowed. Questions about spirituality started to rise up in me. I had become happy thinking of my "church" as the sacredness I could sense in the world, especially in nature, yet I started to think it might be good to give Jeriann a start within a more official religion. My family's faith had little appeal for me, but I knew that Jerry valued his upbringing within the Catholic Church. Even though he had become more secular, and almost never went to Mass, I thought he might like the idea of Jeriann sharing in the faith his family had embraced.

When I told Jerry about my plan, he placed one arm lightly around my shoulders and with his other hand, he pressed ever so lightly on my furrowed brow.

"I don't feel it's necessary to be all that concerned about a particular church," he said. "Nowhere could you find better or more spiritually grounded folks than your mother and father."

I listened, but I decided to follow my instinct and explore Catholicism. I could not imagine raising my daughter with any fire and brimstone, narrow-minded morality, and I had to hope that the Catholic faith was more welcoming. Of course, I knew about the Pope's position on birth control and abortion, but it seemed possible not to throw out the baby with the bathwater. Some parts of Catholicism surely would be helpful to Jeriann as she grew up.

The next day, as soon as Jerry left for work, I telephoned the office of St. Patrick's Cathedral, the magnificent church on Fifth Avenue, and met with the priest the same day.

After a brief conversation, the priest informed me that I would not be eligible for church membership, since my husband and I had divorced. I then asked if Sylvia and Ed Sullivan could be Jeriann's godparents. I explained that Ed was Catholic, and Sylvia Jewish.

"Yes, Mr. Sullivan could be her godfather, but since Mrs. Sullivan is Jewish, it would be against the rules of the Church for her to be godmother."

Disappointed, I walked right out of Saint Patrick's and returned home to get ready for our date at the Pavillon with the Sullivans that evening. During the dinner, Jerry -- with a knowing smile on his face -- spoke of my experience with the priest.

Ed sighed and said, "Well I must say, St. Pat's made an unfortunate decision, because Dean would have been one of their most enthusiastic members."

"Thank you, Ed," I said, "and I also told the priest that I'd rather have Sylvia be Jeriann's godmother than to have the Pope."

Ed threw his head back and laughed heartily, while Sylvia gave me a big hug.

For the moment, I stayed silent about a plan that was swimming around in my head.

The next day I called St. Bartholomew's Episcopal Church at 51st Street and Park Avenue. There I was given a most warm welcome, and a few weeks later the five of us were in the baptism room with a priest. Jeriann, now eleven months old, splashed huge fists of water into Ed's face, causing his laughter to echo into all the sacred corners of the rectory. Ed and Sylvia became Jeriann's godparents. I was now content.

The baby years flew by swiftly. Whether we were in New York for our summers or Miami Beach in winters, each day seemed a miracle of discovery. Perhaps one of our greatest blessings had to do with free time to enjoy our little girl. When Jeriann was about a year old, Jerry's office manager became his assistant, so that Jerry's duties at work were greatly lifted.

The large, colorful toy store, FAO Schwartz, was one of Jeriann's favorite spots nearby. "Daddy, let's go to toys" had, in fact, been Jeriann's first full sentence, one she would utter as she looked pleadingly into the eyes of her adoring Daddy, while pointing in the direction of the door. Often this would be a weekend morning, when Jerry could have slept late. I would see his tan, muscular shoulders as he would change out of his pajamas to go to Schwartz's, and fleetingly I sometimes wished for the days when the shedding of that garment would mean an immediate closeness to me in the bedroom.

Often, our little family of three spent hours adventuring together through the magical aisles of products created by brilliant

264

toy designers. Sometimes I would leave Jeriann and her Daddy in the serious business of selecting toys and books, while I went behind the huge stuffed elephant and closed my eyes to express gratitude that my daughter had these special privileges. I would feel a pang for my dear Daddy and Mommy, remembering how hard they must have found it to watch my sister and me poring over enticing pictures in the Sears Roebuck catalog, knowing they could not afford to buy anything for us. I reminded myself, though, how filled with love and attention our childhoods had been. Jeriann, luckily, was receiving those kinds of gifts too from Jerry and me, and her grandparents in Georgia.

On special occasions, FAO Schwartz came to us, in the form of a box filled with toys and puzzles and picture books. The Schwartz brothers were friends of Jerry's, and often sent presents to her.

Across from FAO Schwartz was Central Park, another of Jeriann's favorite places. We practically lived our summer days on those green lawns, since the outside world of trees and grass delighted Jeriann so much. She enjoyed playing with children from all corners of New York, who came to have fun in the Park. Some of her playmates were African American children from Harlem, some were wealthy white children from the Upper East Side (who were often the children or grandchildren of Jerry's friends, and who came to the Park only with their nannies), and some were simply children from all over New York who had the chance to explore this beautiful green space in the middle of Manhattan. This diverse group of children pleased Jerry and me, because we wanted our daughter to know people of all kinds, and to have an open, welcoming attitude toward everyone.

A problem, however, crept in when Jeriann was three years old, and I feel the solution profoundly affected the course of her life, in the best way imaginable. One of the nannies who often came to the Park spoke to Jerry one morning, as Jeriann raced around with her friends. This nanny was a soft-spoken woman, in charge of the children of one of Jerry's friends, who lived high up in a lovely home overlooking Central Park. She told us that her employers -- and the employers of the other nannies -- felt strongly that their children should not be allowed to play with the children from Harlem or splash and drink from the water fountains where "just anybody drank."

"Mr. Brady, because you permit Jeriann to play with the Harlem kids, who unfortunately are dirty and germy, and you also let her drink from the water fountains, it presents a problem for us."

Jerry responded to this nanny's worries with respect, yet he told her that we wanted Jeriann to mingle with all the children, because we didn't want her to grow up feeling she was better than others. His proclamation concerning the water fountains led some of the nannies to find another area of Central Park for their young charges.

I am convinced that Jerry's stand in this matter was the fertile ground out of which Jeriann's belief in equality and social justice grew. Years later, she would gain a degree in multi-cultural education, and as a teacher and a mother, she nurtures this sense of fairness in her second grade students and her son Brady. Jerry's superb parenting continues to bear valuable fruit.

In Miami Beach too, Jeriann had fun with other children and with her beloved Daddy. She especially loved to swim with Jerry, riding on his back for hours, and jumping into his arms from the edge of the pool. She often came with us to visit friends too.

Her presence even caused a surprising new closeness to spring up with Jerry's brother Fran in Coral Gables. I appreciated those visits to Fran and Anne's house because they were so welcoming of little Jeriann, and gave her a sense of family on Jerry's side, to add to her cherished Georgia family. Fran enjoyed talking about all of the honors he had received, throughout his life, and we spent much time in his trophy room, as he carefully and thoroughly described each item. Jerry and I both tried to be on our best behavior, because we were glad to have this renewed connection in our life, and in the life of our little girl.

Jerry and I often laughed about one of those visits, when we were having dinner at Fran's home in Coral Gables. Fran and Anne excitedly showed us a recent painting they had bought. It looked abstract and I couldn't figure out what to say about it, but I just kept busy exclaiming over it so they would not see the bored look on Jerry's face.

As we ate a six course meal, served by maids, Jeriann, who was now eighteen months old, became restless, so her daddy let her crawl on the plush white carpets. Soon I was horrified to see she had made her way to the most cherished piece of furniture our "blueblood" relatives owned: a washstand Fran and Anne had brought back from Italy, believing it to have originally been Cleopatra's. Jeriann had crawled under it and was flicking bits of paint off the bottom of the deeply indented wash bowl, encased in an elegant cabinet.

Immediately I collected her and put her Daddy in charge of keeping her out of mischief while I quietly picked up the bits she had tweaked off and put them in my purse to discard later. I hoped my relatives had not noticed what had happened to their prized possession.

Returning home later that evening in our white Thunderbird convertible, with Jeriann sitting in her daddy's lap as he drove (believe it or not, in those days it was not illegal to drive with your child in your lap!), I decided to tell Jerry about our little girl's mischief-making.

"Jerry, did you see Jeriann crawl under that precious washstand of Cleopatra's and flick the old paint off? I was mortified when I noticed her."

I realized, as I said this, that my annoyance at Jeriann's behavior had faded, and I felt indescribably happy as we cruised down Collins Avenue.

Jerry smiled. "Yes, and didn't the old cabinet look ever so much better after her refinishing work!"

With Jerry's eyes looking straight ahead, our little girl absorbed in her power behind the wheel, and Jerry's profile highlighting his princely nose, we reached home and came to a stop in our driveway.

In thinking back to those exciting years, it seems unusual that Jeriann was about two years old before we arranged for a visit so Jerry and my parents could meet. Many times after Jerry's phone conversations with them he would comment that they must meet sometime. Jeriann and I went back and forth frequently from New York to Ellijay, including a couple or more weeks during the Christmas season, on our way to our winter home in Miami. We always visited Georgia in early spring, to enjoy the planting season, but Jerry was too busy at that time of year overseeing the crew transporting his tote board equipment from the Florida winter racing tracks to New York summer tracks. Whenever Jerry and I invited my parents to come and visit us, they would say that much as they would love to meet Jerry, they were reluctant to leave home. Since Jerry and I shared affectionate, warm conversations with my parents each week, it seemed that he and my Mommy and Daddy had already met.

During the year of Jeriann's second Christmas season, we made plans for Jeriann and Mommy to spend their March birthdays together in Miami. So the last week in February, Jeriann and I flew to Georgia and then had a very fun leisurely drive with Mommy and Daddy back to Miami. Jerry paid all the expenses and we spent a few days in lovely hotel rooms in various towns along the way. Each time we entered a new town, Daddy would say, "I've often read about this town in the *Georgia Market Bulletin*."

This traveling was a new experience for my parents, but it would soon become "old hat," since they made several more visits to both New York and Miami during those years. Jerry had them come to New York during the World's Fair, of course with all expenses paid.

Even though they loved their visits, it was quite visible to me they worried a great deal about their animals and the home place, even though Jerry paid a neighbor to stay in their house and take care of the farm while they were away. He always thought of everything that would make life more comfortable for them.

Jerry was excited and thrilled each time we coaxed them to visit. He so enjoyed their responses to everything around them. At the winner's circle at the race tracks, he loved how Daddy would be close to giggles as he watched people place necklaces of roses around the sleek, well-groomed horse's neck. During all their visits, as we walked together to restaurants and to a variety of sights, Jerry walked with Mommy and ever so tenderly held her elbow. He wanted to put my hard working parents up in luxury hotels, but this was the one area where I had to disagree, for my parents' sake.

"I want them to have rooms overlooking the big ocean," Jerry exclaimed.

"No, they wouldn't be comfortable in a fancy place," I would say. Often I made their reservation in a retirement community setting, instead of a hotel, and they enjoyed themselves in those peaceful, quiet places.

That first March birthday for Jeriann and Mommy was a real hoot for us all. As we had a festive dinner at Nick and Arthur's Steak House, we noticed a large party hosted by one of Jerry's friends, a prominent racing stable owner. Coincidentally, that large family was celebrating their mother's birthday and her name was also Mamie. I don't think I ever saw Mommy laugh more delightedly than she did that evening, when the waiter joined our two tables so that both family groups could cut cakes together and sing Happy Birthday to the two Mamies.

Daddy nudged me with his elbow and said, "I'll never be able to live with your mother on the farm, after she has experienced all this!"

Year by year my happiness multiplied until I felt my heart could not contain it, but like everything in this human scene of existence -- nothing stays the same . . .

PART III

Home Again to Yonder Mountain

Figure 14: Jerry and Jeriann playing in the pool in Miami Beach

19: Our Last Days with Jerry

The date was January 15, 1965, a bright, sunny day typical of many of the glorious winter days Jerry and I spent together during all the years at our winter home in Miami Beach. This day was destined to be different, however.

It began for Jeriann and her Dad with a rousing play period in our pool. Jerry had by this time retired from his job and spent much of his time with Jeriann and me. I watched from a second floor window, enjoying their antics while I kept one eye on the clock, so as to get Jerry to his doctor's appointment on time. Jerry had been feeling more tired than usual, and losing more weight than seemed right. I had seen him often rubbing his back, as if he had a constant pain, although he always brushed off my worries with a cheerful "I'm sure it's nothing, Deany."

The verdict from the doctor was inoperable cancer.

I remember being in Dr. Kaye's office when he told us the news. I sat facing his desk with Sylvia on my right side and another dear friend, Rose Shirley, on my left. In those days, the patient heard the diagnosis after the family, and only if the family thought it was best for them to know.

I don't remember anything else the doctor said that day. I do remember that both Sylvia and Rose grabbed each of my hands at

275

the same moment when Dr. Kaye said "cancer." After that I couldn't hear what he was saying. I could only focus on those hands that held tightly to my own. I remember thinking how Sylvia's hands were so strong and big, out of proportion to her slender body, and how Rose's hands were so smooth. Funny what the mind latches onto.

Those first few months were a blur. Sylvia and Ed convinced me that Jerry should know, so I told him. Jerry resisted treatment, with the support of his doctor. Although new developments had been happening in the field of chemotherapy, Dr. Kaye was suspicious of them, and in any case the cancer had already spread.

I tried putting Jeriann in preschool to give Jerry some rest in the mornings. On the first morning of school, however, Jeriann wrapped her entire body around Jerry's leg and clung to him, crying and begging not to go.

Jerry turned to me and said, "I can't do this." And that was the end of preschool.

During the next year, before Jerry got too sick, we had many precious days together as I savored moments of poignant joy with my Prince. He played with Jeriann every chance he could, as if to make up for all the times he would not have to play with her in the future. Once I saw him listening with a tear on his cheek to the song "Turn Around" by Harry Belafonte.

Where are you going, my little one, little one,
Where are you going, my baby, my own?

. . .

Turn around and you're tiny,

Turn around and you're grown,

Turn around and you're a young wife with babes of your
own.

Jeriann asks me now if Jerry and I talked about dying. Like most couples back then, we didn't discuss things as directly as people do now. We simply tried to be strong for each other. When sad thoughts would start to come, I just choked them back. Jerry and I held each other tightly after we made love, but we never talked about death.

In a surprising way, our love grew deeper during those three and a half years of Jerry's sickness. I thanked God for all the joy this man had brought into my life. As Jerry grew helpless, I found I could give him comfort, and that knowledge gave me strength. I remember he once said, "Please don't let this horrible illness be the way you remember me." I got through the last months knowing that helping him now was the one thing I could do to thank him for rescuing me when my life was at its lowest.

Once, as I helped Jerry to the bathroom, he said, "Where would I be now if I had never met you?"

I just looked deep into his pain-filled eyes and said, "But where would *I* be if I had never met *you*?"

And yet there were times when my heart would break, as I stood by in helpless agony, witnessing Jerry's suffering. Growing concerned that his illness and my sadness were becoming overwhelming for Jeriann, I brought her as often as possible to my Mommy and Daddy, so they could look after her and give her more cheerful days in the fresh air and sunshine of the countryside. She loved her "Best Mama and Pop" very much, and I hoped she didn't realize how sick her Daddy was.

Jerry had been the one to suggest this term of endearment, "Best Mama," which Jeriann had happily adopted. Jerry had been in bed one day, and I had been crying as I sat on the bed next to him, when I said about my mother, "She is the best Mama."

To which Jerry had said with a smile, "How about that being how Jeriann refers to her grandma, as 'Best Mama'?"

By the time Jerry and I left our winter home in Miami Beach in the spring of 1968, Jerry's health was severely failing. If I had known then that I would never return with him and Jeriann to our home in Florida, it would have been traumatic. Sometimes, for the sake of mental stability, the truth must unfold gradually and by merciful degrees.

I had suggested to Jerry -- because of a phone conversation I had had with his New York doctor -- that this would be a good time for Jeriann to visit her Best Mama and Pop in Georgia, possibly for the summer. I would bring her to them, and then head straight back to New York to take care of Jerry. Jerry agreed reluctantly, saying he wanted the best for her, but he would really miss her.

Jeriann felt the same way, and at the airport, she started to cry. Jerry hugged and kissed his little girl, saying, "Darling baby, don't cry. I hope it's going to be only a few short weeks until I see you at home again in New York."

I managed to keep the tears from flowing until Jeriann and I were seated comfortably in the plane headed for Atlanta. Soon after we were airborne, Jeriann fell asleep with her head on a pillow. I started to cry as I remembered the phone conversation I had had the week before with Jerry's New York doctor, Dr. Hiller.

"Now, Dean, please don't get upset," Dr. Hiller had said. "I advise you, though, to leave Jeriann with your parents for the coming summer months, because Dr. Kaye shared the results of some tests he ran in Miami. We never come to conclusions without more tests, though, and we can certainly have more done when Jerry arrives back here in New York."

Looking out the window of the airplane, I quietly sobbed. I had had to appear strong and calm for Jerry and Jeriann, yet I felt overwhelmed at the thought of what was to come.

Jeriann and I stayed in Georgia for a week. Once she was calm and happy, nesting in my parents' loving home, I flew back to New York. Dr. Hiller did more tests for Jerry, and suggested a medical route to slow the progress of the cancer. I thought Jerry would say no, but after three and a half years of resisting medical intervention, Jerry agreed to submit to surgery and other treatments. All of this was terribly hard on Jerry physically, however, as one

279

thing led to another, and throughout the summer, the nightmare kept escalating, day by day, with heartbreak too painful to remember and relate.

On top of our own troubles, the whole nation sometimes appeared to be collapsing during that spring and summer of 1968, with the assassination on April 4th of Martin Luther King, Jr., and then the assassination on June 6th of Robert F. Kennedy -- a tragedy following the earlier murder of his brother President John F. Kennedy in 1962, the year of Jeriann's birth. My dinner companion Joe Kennedy was in delicate health, having suffered a stroke a few years earlier, and he would die that November. People -- especially young people -- were increasingly protesting the American war in Vietnam and the military draft. The air was filled with questioning and change. As I sat by Jerry's bed, I couldn't help feeling that the whole world was suffering. I had so much distress of my own, though, that I could barely manage to keep up with the news. Even our close friendships languished, because all I could do was to focus on Jerry.

Jeriann's summer on the farm was a great blessing for us all. June and July brought a huge crop of blackberries along the rich creek bank. My Mommy and Daddy's letters and phone calls glowed with accounts of the fun Jeriann was enjoying as she rode piggy-back on her Pop's back and reached the luscious berries that grew wild on the edges of fields. Frequently Jeriann invited all my family to join her when she returned to her Daddy in New York. It was a dream none of us could interrupt with the sad facts.

Jeriann, however, thought about her Daddy's illness all summer. Luckily, she had her Best Mama and Pop to talk with about her sadness. They always approached questions of family life with honesty and care. On one of her piggy-back blackberry excursions, she asked my Dad a question.

"Pop, is my Daddy going to die?"

As Daddy would tell me many times during his remaining years, at this point he had eased Jeriann off his back and sat down with her on a nearby tree stump. He expected to reach for her and take her onto his lap, but instead she took her trembling hands and dug her little fingers into his lap. She stared straight into his eyes, appearing to be deeply pondering what his answer would be.

"Honey," my Dad told her, "sometimes people have to die and leave this world and we cannot understand why. It looks like it is your dear Daddy's time to die."

Jeriann broke into sobs, burying her face in his lap. As my Dad told it later, his tears fell onto her sweet little head as he patted her back, and they cried together for quite some time.

Then she raised her body again and with her fingers digging into the tops of his legs so hard that her fingers were pinching the flesh, she asked, "Will you be my Daddy now?"

"Yes, my darling child, I'll be a Daddy to you just as I am to your Mommy. I'll be with you every day as you grow up. I could never replace your own Daddy, though I'll do my best. Of course, I cannot give you a fancy kind of city life like your Daddy did."

Her response came through choking sobs. "I don't want a fancy city life! I want a Daddy."

Soon her grandfather lifted her to stand on the tree stump and she went piggyback again. He described later how he could feel her limp little body, with her heartbeats quieter now. He walked home, carrying Jeriann on his back, and together they felt welcomed by the comforting smells of cornbread baking in the oven and green beans simmering on the stove. Best Mama's arms stretched out to hold Jeriann in a warm embrace.

He always ended the story in this way:

"All the way down the mountain to home, I prayed hard for the good Lord to give me strength to be a pop who was like a daddy to her."

In the last week of August, Colleen brought Jeriann with her from Georgia to New York. Colleen had agreed to nurse Jerry and administer his injections so he could live his last months at home instead of at the hospital. We had worked out these arrangements in advance, but I dreaded my sister's arrival, because I knew this signaled the end. Colleen, in fact, insisted on coming about two weeks before I was ready. I understood that she wanted to ease Jerry's last days, and I knew she was right, yet I couldn't help wishing for just a little more time on my own with him.

However, as soon as Colleen was with us, it became clear that both Jerry and I needed her very much. The gift of her presence those last couple of months was a treasure for which I will be eternally grateful. Colleen and Jerry had always been fond of each other, and her sensible, pragmatic nature was just what he needed at that time. She nursed Jerry tirelessly, in addition to keeping our home running smoothly at a time when I didn't feel capable of doing it. Sometimes I felt like I couldn't even find air to breathe and I just needed to get outside. Colleen would urge me to take a walk and have some moments of peace.

The love between Jerry and Jeriann continued, growing in strength each day, yet I continued to worry about Jeriann. She started to tiptoe around our apartment, as if she worried that any noise might make her Daddy worse. She liked to play on the floor near his bed. Often, if she was busy elsewhere, Jerry would ask to see her, and his face always lit up with smiles as soon as she came into the room.

One day in October, he called to me from his bed.

"Deany, please bring Jeriann and her little red rocker to sit beside my bed."

I brought her there and he reached his thin arm to pull her closer against the side of his bed.

"My darling little girl, Jeriann," he said, "I hope you grow up to be a sweet, warm and loving woman like your mother."

On the morning of October 17, 1968, a slight smile flickered across Jerry's face and his kind blue eyes sparkled briefly as he looked into my eyes. I embraced him, holding my heart to his heart, and he drew his last breath.

20: The Year After

The year after Jerry's death was the most difficult of my life. In addition to coping with my own grief, I felt concerned about Jeriann's emotional health. I also started to realize that I was making choices financially that were creating a bewildering mess. Gradually, all that I had shared with Jerry -- our love, our home together, our happiness -- seemed to disappear, along with the financial security Jerry had worked so hard to establish.

At the heart of the problem was the fashion business I had started. During the last year of his life, Jerry had encouraged me to take some classes in business and fashion. There I had met a woman named Masako, a fashion designer originally from Japan. I was impressed with her focus and determination, and made plans to open a dress shop with her.

By the time I decided to do this, Jerry was too sick to advise me. I was frantic to create a life for myself in New York, knowing that I would have to face being on my own soon, yet my business sense is not my strongest talent in the best of times. I had no knowledge of how to run a shop, especially in the ultra-competitive world of Manhattan fashion.

After Jerry's death, I poured money from his estate into renovating an old shop on Madison Avenue, with the help of an architect I hired to design the large storefront with a fancy style similar to Joan Gaines' salon in Miami Beach. Masako and I then opened Jerry Brady Fashions Dress Salon, a high-end shop where we designed, made, and sold custom-fitted dresses and ball gowns. I furnished the money, greeted customers and did the selling, while Masako designed the outfits. Her two daughters and two professional seamstresses sewed the garments in a back room, under Masako's strict eye.

One of the biggest mistakes I made, from the start, was to ignore the sound advice of Ed Sullivan and Nat Herzfeld, the Executors of Jerry's estate, who urged me not to rush into a partnership with Masako, especially in such a risky business. Without thinking it through, I plunged ahead and created this partnership, even granting Masako the same authority as I had to write checks. Ed and Nat had been right. As quickly as Masako and I put money into our shop, we lost it.

Although Sylvia and other celebrity friends often came to the store at first, and tried to help me gain customers, gradually the customers started to vanish, and I was left worrying over how to pay for materials and rent. Masako, as I came to discover, was an insensitive business partner, who started to show her uglier side even to the well-heeled women who came into the shop. I started to feel that I had jumped blindly onto a runaway horse, and I had no idea how to make it stop, before it threw me to the ground.

Another mistake I made was in naming the shop after Jerry,

simply because I was determined to honor him. Ed and Nat reminded me that using Jerry's name wasn't appropriate, since his career and interests had nothing to do with women's fashions.

My psychiatrist was another concerned person to whom I rarely listened. He diagnosed me as having severe depression with bipolar tendencies. He urged me to stay in therapy, and for awhile I did -- especially because Sylvia Sullivan had given both Jeriann and me the gift of therapy sessions. I found it too difficult to continue the therapy, though, because I couldn't face my life with honesty then. I had started to drink much too heavily, and this too I tried to hide from those who cared about me. The awful combination of alcohol and antidepressants added to my problems.

At that painful time, in fact, I avoided anyone who tried to tell me what to do. My mental state at that time inclined toward a mild state of paranoia, especially regarding Ed and Nat. To this day, I have never been able to erase from my mind the image of their concerned expressions when we discussed my partner Masako. It is a sad fact that the one person I should have resisted and refused to listen to was Masako herself.

In the midst of this confusion, I cherished moments of normalcy in my life with Jeriann. She especially loved continuing traditions she and Jerry had created, from special breakfasts to adventures at the Zoo. I especially wanted to create a sense of calmness and happiness for Jeriann because I had become worried about her in the months leading up to and following Jerry's death.

She had started to eat very little, and her teachers said she hardly ever spoke. Even around me she sat silent much of the time. In first grade so far, she had not learned to read a single word. She was having as much trouble in school, in fact, as she was at home, and that year I would change her school three times, hoping to find a better environment for her. The psychiatrist told me that sometimes Jeriann didn't seem quite sure of her surroundings, and often sat in his office without talking or playing with any of the toys he brought out for her. I wished I could just let her live in Georgia for a while with her Best Mama and Pop, but I worried about taking her out of her first year of school, especially since she was already so far behind.

One Sunday I woke up early, determined to do all I could to help bring a sense of comfort and certainty back into my life with Jeriann. I made her a big breakfast of grits and egg -- her favorite. She just picked at the food, though, and after I washed our dishes, I realized that she was sitting still, with her hands folded, in a straight-back chair, staring vacantly out the window. After trying to persuade Jeriann to play with her toys and puzzles, I mustered my best effort at faking joy.

"Come, Jeriann, let's go to FAO Schwartz! You always love that store. We'll find you something great today."

That did bring a smile to her sad face. Minutes later we were on our way, hand in hand, skipping the few blocks to the store's entrance on Fifth Avenue. Walking into the cheerful store for the first time since Jerry's death, however, I felt overwhelmed by a wave of sadness. Now that wonderful Daddy, who rushed to give both Jeriann and me everything our hearts desired, was gone. Yet, looking at the smile on my daughter's face, I knew I had to swallow my tears and make this a fun time for her.

An hour or so later, our arms loaded with packages as we headed down 58th Street to our apartment, we passed a sweet little florist shop -- especially sweet to me, because Jerry used to stop there and bring me fresh flowers daily.

Jeriann asked happily, "Can we stop and get flowers?"

"Yes, let's get black-eyed Susans for your huge brown eyes."

As we browsed through the large variety of bright, sweet-smelling flowers, I called to Jeriann.

"Come, dear one, and sit with me while I tell you a story about you and your Daddy."

I found a comfortable chair in a quiet corner of the shop, and Jeriann climbed up into my lap. I remembered all the times my Grandma or Mommy would hold me on their laps and tell me stories. It felt good to realize I could comfort Jeriann as they had comforted me.

"Almost from the first time I met your Daddy, he loved to have a vase of fresh flowers. He would buy flowers from this very shop on his way home from work each day, and once he got home, the first thing he did after giving you and me a warm hug was to care for the flowers."

Jeriann looked around the flower shop, her face brightening, as if she felt comforted being where she knew her Daddy had spent time.

"Your Daddy had a daily adventure discovering all about you, when you were little. He knew that one of your favorite things was to be held high up in his arms as he walked around our apartment. You especially loved it when he would stand in front of the mirror, swaying back and forth while you looked at yourself and your Daddy in the reflection. The mirror was right over the spot with the vase of flowers.

"Then one day, to his surprise, you reached over and ate one of the flowers!"

Jeriann giggled. "I did?"

"Yes, you did! You ate it right up! and Daddy was terribly worried that you would be poisoned."

Jeriann's eyes widened. "Was I okay?"

I hugged her and laughed. "Yes, the doctor said you would be okay. But your daddy wasn't going to take any chances! He said you and I were better than fresh flowers any day, and he had to keep us healthy! So he made sure to keep our household free of flowers from then on."

At bedtime that night Jeriann asked me to repeat the story again and again. Afterward, she chirped like a little bird, "Oh Mommy, Mommy, I love Daddy!" and she rolled on the bed laughing. Her happy energy started a pillow fight, and I couldn't get enough of her giggles. This was the first time I had heard her laugh so much since she and Jerry had played together before Jerry had gotten too sick.

Once I had kissed Jeriann goodnight and tucked her into bed, I found myself alone. I walked into the living room and opened the liquor cabinet to get the bottle of Scotch. Bringing ice and a glass from the kitchen, I settled myself, sinking deeply into the plush living room chair with my drink, the bottle of Scotch on the table beside me. For three or four hours, as usual, I tried to drown my loneliness, grief, and anxiety.

It became clear, in the course of that year that I couldn't afford to go on in New York. I found it too hard to face this fact, however. My family pleaded with me daily by phone to come back to the farm so they could help me raise my daughter in a healthier atmosphere. I had left Georgia, though, and did not want to be driven back by failure.

Most midnights I was able to make it to the big bed to lie beside our beautiful, peacefully sleeping daughter, before I became unconscious.

21: My Friendship with Sylvia

On a spring day in 1969, after many cancellations on my part, I was about to have lunch at The Plaza Hotel with Sylvia Sullivan. For months, since Jerry's death, I had been cancelling each date with her, because I just could not face her seeing me in such a pitiful situation as I was in now.

Sylvia, like Ed, intensely disliked my business partner, believing that Masako had brought only difficulty into my life. I knew in my heart they were right, yet I could not acknowledge it. In the space of half a year, I had wasted a good portion of my daughter's inheritance, which her father had spent a lifetime investing sensibly.

Sylvia had tried to share her observations with me, in order to protect me from this situation with Masako. As she said once, "I've never seen a partnership where the partners were as far apart in their thinking as you two. Dean, it seems it crushes you to have to talk assertively with a customer, but Masako appears to get energy from being high handed with even the nicest customers, and I've seen her fire seamstresses and I watched them leave, crying. She has the most abrasive personality I've ever seen."

Sylvia actually didn't know how awful this situation with Masako had become. I could never have told her how cruel my partner could be to her own daughters, forcing them to work long hours, or how she tried to persuade me to marry her son-in-law, so that he could gain United States citizenship. She told me I was selfish not to agree to a "simple ceremony" like this, now that I was a widow. She even hinted at threatening me if I did not comply with a paper marriage. I depended on Masako's expertise in clothing design, however, and thought she was important to the business, so I tried to ignore how she pushed me and other people around.

As I approached the Plaza that spring day, I thought about Jeriann, who was at a new school nearby. She had been struggling through many teary bouts in her classroom, grieving for her Daddy. Jeriann also worried about me. Once when she had gone on a playdate she asked her friend's mother to telephone me, because she was worried I might be sad without her. I hoped Sylvia wouldn't question me too closely about Jeriann. I knew she would be upset if she found out that Jeriann and I had stopped going to the therapist Sylvia and Ed had funded.

Walking slowly up the steps of the elegant Plaza, I remembered all the gala events the Sullivans and Jerry and I had enjoyed together at the hotel restaurant, often in a cozy corner -- usually just the four of us. I noticed some young people sitting nearby on the sidewalk, with their long hair, the women wearing flowing Indian print skirts. One of the boys was playing a guitar and singing, while the others smoked cigarettes and talked. I felt old for a moment, even though I was just forty-one. I wondered fleetingly what my own girlhood would have been like, if I had had the independence and freedom these young people seemed to have today.

"Deany, dear," a familiar voice called. I turned and waved to Sylvia, who rushed to join me at the door of the Plaza. The fact that she called me "Deany" was a surprise, because she always called me Dean. "Deany" had been only Jerry's special name for me.

Sylvia wore a crisp linen dress with huge orange poppies on a white background -- the picture of a chic, mature model, and the opposite of a hippie! Something I had always admired about Sylvia was that she had such a clear, simple style, in any season and at any time of day. At luncheons, she usually wore custom-tailored dresses like this one, bright with splashy flowers. I wondered if she would ever change.

She hugged me tenderly but firmly, as we walked close together into the lobby. A great many people were gathering, getting organized for lunch in the large dining room just off one side of the lobby. We were headed for the smaller, more intimate dining room on the opposite side.

Once we were seated, Sylvia said, "Ed and I have been missing you. Tell me how you and our little godchild Jeriann have been?"

She had placed a Coco Chanel shopping bag on the seat beside her and I imagined it was another Paris original for Jeriann. Sylvia's enormous brown eyes, so familiar to me now, were smiling as she handed the shopping bag across the table to me, saying, "It's in a Chanel bag, but it's really designed by a children's clothing store where I bought clothes for Betty when she was small."

I was touched, and tears welled in my eyes as I said, "When my Grandma was stretching the cheap fabric to barely get two dresses for my sister and me, she never dreamed that my daughter would be wearing Paris originals from the time she was a baby!"

Sylvia squeezed my hand much as Jerry had so often done. As she bowed her head, I felt she was saying a prayer for me and Jerry's most adored daughter.

I wanted to tell her that Jeriann was just fine, but I couldn't get that lie to pass my lips.

"Jeriann is doing alright," I said. "School is a little hard for her right now."

"Are you both still seeing the family psychologist that Ed suggested?"

"Yes," I lied, as I dropped my eyes, pretending to look at the list of h'ors-d'oeuvres on the menu.

Glancing up from the menu, I saw a pained expression shoot from Sylvia's eyes as she looked out the window behind me, facing Central Park South. I sensed she wanted to hear more about Jeriann but felt I was too fragile, so she changed the subject.

"Are you still fond of shrimp Alfredo, Dean?"

I nodded yes, and she reached across the table to pat my hand.

"It's still my favorite food in Italian restaurants," I said, "but today I think I'll have a cup of borscht." I really just wanted a salad, but felt so weak and trembly; I didn't think I had the energy to chew.

Sylvia probably knew I was lying and holding myself at a distance, but she kept reaching out to me. She smiled again so indulgently, in fact, that I almost broke down and cried. I quickly got hold of my emotions, however, and kept up my barrier.

I could only take a few spoonfuls of the soup. Watching me, Sylvia said, with an effort at humor, "You know all us women loved you dearly, but we couldn't help being a little envious of how you could eat all those calories and not gain an ounce."

Again feeling her tender love, as I did on the night we first met at the Post and Paddock Restaurant in Miami Beach, I bit my lip to stay calm.

"Sylvia, you will never know how much I appreciate you taking me under your wing, and in that way you encouraged all our friends into an unconditional acceptance of me -- I must have seemed like a little wayfaring waif, who had entered Jerry's life."

"Precious Dean, I don't think you will ever realize how wonderful you really are. You are an inspiration to us all. Jerry was from the beginning so in love with you, and you and Jeriann gave him a near perfect life."

297

I wanted to bottle her words, because somehow I felt I would never hear them again. I couldn't find any words of my own, though, and Sylvia must have given up in despair, as I sat in my chair looking at the tablecloth. She tried to cover over this awkward moment by pretending to be giddily cheerful, as she invited me to an upcoming celebration. Her artificial tone was so unlike her usual sincerity, though, that I must have winced.

"Dear Dean, we have some celebrating to do in a couple of weeks! So many of Ed's friends -- including you! -- were unable to attend our First Anniversary of the dedication of Ed's theater, in December, so Ed and I are having another celebration. I hope you'll join us, Dean!"

Sylvia was talking about the famous theater up on Broadway, which used to be called Studio 50. After many years of holding *The Ed Sullivan Show* there, Ed had been honored with a dedication of this theater in his name -- the Ed Sullivan Theater.

"Sure, I will be honored to be there." I tried to sound enthusiastic.

"Lovely! and you can bring your partner."

She dropped her voice to almost a whisper and gazed again out the window behind me. I knew she was having a hard time expressing pleasure at the thought of Masako.

When the waiter approached our table, Sylvia asked for the check. As he headed toward the cash desk with her charge card, she leaned across the table toward me and said, "Tell me, how is your lovely family in Georgia?"

"They're on the phone constantly, begging me to come back home."

"Oh, I know they would love to have you and Jeriann with them."

I vigorously shook my head from side to side. I couldn't imagine giving up and leaving this city I had lived in so happily with Jerry. I couldn't imagine going back to Georgia.

"Honestly, dear, that wouldn't be a bad idea," Sylvia said. "There's nothing like family. I have lost so many members of my own family, and I often think how comforting it would be to see them again."

Once Sylvia had signed for the tip, she took out her little personal address book, and opened it to my page. With her blunt and large-knuckled fingers, she pointed to the many crossed out numbers. Seeing her hands, I thought again how much prettier my mother's work-worn hands were than those manicured ones of Sylvia's.

Holding two fingers on the page of her address book, Sylvia said, "Dear, this concerns me that you have changed your telephone number eight times since October."

Again, I couldn't think what to say. I had changed my number so that I would be inaccessible to friends, even close friends like Sylvia. She placed the address book back in her purse, and we walked outside into the New York sunshine. Across 59th Street, the trees in Central Park were just starting to come into leaf. Small children were walking toward the Park, holding the hands of parents and nannies. Sylvia and I were quiet as we walked toward my apartment building. In a couple of blocks we passed The Earl Kelley School, where Jeriann was in first grade.

Sylvia said, with a touch of hopefulness, "Why don't we drop in and I could get a hug and give Jeriann this little present?"

"Sylvia, I am quite sure that at this hour, on this day, the children would be at a children's gym a few blocks down the street."

I hoped to God it was true that this was the gym day, because Sylvia looked so disappointed. I knew I just had to get to my apartment soon, so that I could mix myself a double Scotch and water, lie down, and black out the memory of the past two hours before I picked up Jeriann at the end of the school day.

At our apartment door, Sylvia said to the doorman, "Hello, Mike, you're looking well!"

Bowing, he said, "It's always so good to see you, Mrs. Sullivan."

Sylvia and I hugged briefly as the elevator came to a stop at the ground floor.

"Ed will be thrilled to see you at the party," she said. "We're counting on you, Dean!"

I waved to her as I stepped into the elevator.

"I'll be there," I said. "Thank you, Sylvia, for everything, and see you soon!"

That lunch date, however, proved to be the last time I would see Sylvia. It was our last goodbye.

22: Cold Hard Cement

The day following my lunch with Sylvia, Jeriann and I took our usual walk of four blocks to her school. I couldn't shake the jolt of Sylvia's suggestion that I should go back to Georgia. After kissing Jeriann goodbye, I walked home, stamping my feet hard on the cement as I pushed past a group of slow moving tourists excitedly exclaiming about the sights.

Entering my apartment building, I said to myself, "Enough! Enough of that sentimental stuff about going home to the farm. I'll show Mommy and Daddy and all of them! I've won so many battles, against all odds, to get to this point in my life, and I will again. I'll turn things around and make my business a huge success."

With all my best efforts, however, I could not succeed with the dress shop. I became so discouraged; I had no idea what to do.

The day had come for the party at the Ed Sullivan Theater, and I had kept busy from morning to afternoon working in our boutique. I dreaded the evening and fervently wished I had not promised Sylvia I'd attend. I thought of pretending I had come down with a virus, but since I had already told Masako and her teenage daughters Mari and Yuki they could join me, I felt obliged to go.

I had found a highly recommended babysitter to spend the night with Jeriann. Claudette had been the nanny for the children of the Prime Minister of Canada, so I trusted that Jeriann would be fine with her. I knew too that Jeriann and I needed to be separate at times. Yet we had been together almost each night since Jerry's passing, and I felt anxious about this change.

Masako and her daughters were late joining me outside our shop on Madison Avenue. As usual, Masako took the lead as we entered the taxicab, rushing to sit up front with the driver as the girls sandwiched me between them. Giggling and joyfully patting my back, they seemed unaware of their mother's irritation with this display of affection. That spring, while Masako and I had been desperately hanging on and hoping for a miraculous change in our business, she had started to run the back room like a sweatshop, keeping her daughters and the other two seamstresses sewing day and night. Lately I had not seen the girls in a relaxed setting. Masako ruled them with an iron hand, accompanied by screams and yells.

Masako, in fact, had practically banned my earlier, warm relationship with Mari and Yuki. Although at the beginning of our partnership, she had insisted that the girls address me as Auntie Dean, recently they had told me their mother had forbidden them to call me this anymore. Now, when Yuki's happy tone came out melodiously, "Auntie Dean, it's so good to be going somewhere with you again," her mother flinched. In a stern voice, she gave the driver the address of the Ed Sullivan Theater, Broadway and West 53rd. She kept turning her head to glare at all of us with her angry, piercing eyes.

Times Square and midtown Manhattan were crowded, as our taxicab slowly maneuvered its way up toward the Theater in fits and starts. We asked the driver to let us off a few blocks away, because of the traffic, and we arrived so late that we missed the speeches and toasts. I could not even see Sylvia or Ed in the crowd of well-dressed, fashionable people. Many friends greeted me -- Jerry's dear friends, who hugged me and squeezed my hand in wordless sympathy. Several parties would be going on afterward at fancy restaurants and clubs, and various friends invited me, but I knew I wanted just to lose myself and be alone. At one point, Frank Sinatra and a stunning girlfriend moved toward me, his blue eyes registering pain. As he hugged me, he whispered into my ear, "We'll see you soon, Dean, since we're also at Sylvia and Ed's table." I did not search for their table, though. Instead, I hovered on the margins of all this festivity. Although I was not ready to accept the full truth of it, New York without Jerry did not feel like my home anymore. I could not be with the people who reminded me of Jerry. I could not face my failure to succeed without him. I felt more than ever like the girl from Appalachia planning her own drowning in the waters of Miami Beach.

Before I could gain my bearings, the happy guests started to pour out into the lobby and to find cabs and limos to their after-parties. Outside the theater, as the crowd swept us along to the sidewalk, I said goodbye to Masako and her daughters. I told them friends would be picking me up and bringing me to a party, although I knew I was headed for a quiet, intimate Chinese restaurant on Lexington Avenue, where Jerry and I had spent so many evenings together in our corner booth. During those years, after a couple of hours or so, we would saunter home to our apartment, hand in hand. I had not had a meal there in well over a year, because Jerry had been so ill, and I almost never went out on my own.

Upon entering the restaurant, I paused at the reservation desk and asked to use their phone to call home. Jeriann answered, and her warm, caring voice felt like a sweet mountain breeze.

"Hello Mommy. I miss you."

"I miss you too, my angel baby. Where's Mrs. Claudette?"

"Here she is. I love you Mommy."

"And how I love you, my precious one. You are my life."

Claudette's heavy, warm French accent and kind words comforted me. All my fears about Jeriann's safety were put to rest, and I told Claudette I would be home soon.

The restaurant was peaceful and uncrowded, unlike the chaotic atmosphere on Broadway. Even though the manager was not the man Jerry and I had known in the restaurant in earlier years, he surprised me by leading me to the corner booth where we had always sat.

Soon the waiter came to take my order. I had no appetite for food, and hastily decided this would be a martini night for me. During past years I would order a Scotch sour before dinner, while Jerry occasionally had one small sherry. I had not had a martini since that fateful night when I had allowed the used car salesman to seduce me in the Biltmore Hotel in Atlanta, almost twenty years earlier. I don't know what possessed me to ask the waiter to bring me that drink now. Even more recklessly, I told him a couple of my friends were coming down from their rooms in the hotel above, and they too would like martinis. Soon there were three martinis lined up in front of me.

I asked for the check ahead of time, saying, "I would like to pay now. In that way, I can be sure I'm treating my friends, with no arguing about the bill."

My plan was to drink the martinis down and then walk the two blocks to our apartment. I placed my bag on the table to hide the other martinis and began to drink the first one. The taste was bitter and odd, but I knew martinis were powerful, and something powerfully mind-changing was what I needed on that sad night. After gulping down two of them, I began to feel strange. By the time I gulped down my third martini, the room started to swirl.

Closing my eyes to help with the dizziness, I imagined I could feel Jerry's familiar pat on my shoulder. I remembered so vividly being with him at *The Ed Sullivan Show,* the night Elvis had been on stage. All the same sights, sounds of applause and shouts were playing over again in my mind. The colors were there too, especially the pinkness of Ed's sweet and familiar face, animated with the inward thrill he always showed when he knew he was creating television history. The precious warmth and smell of Jerry sitting beside me felt real and so comforting. I relived the moment when I had told Jerry I was proud of Elvis, as a "down home boy" who had made it big, and how Jerry had said, "You and those down home boys certainly know how to use your fannies." I could just hear Ed describing Elvis as a "thoroughly nice boy," and Jerry laughing with me, as we remembered Ed's note saying how Dean Brady was "a thoroughly nice girl."

In this dreamy, martini-induced state, I felt myself overflowing with joy as I relived all the shimmering scenes in Ed's theater, with The Beatles, The Supremes, Joan Rivers, Stevie Wonder, and many more entertainers. With Jerry by my side, I had felt relaxed and right at home, no matter how filled the theater had been with celebrities. All of it had felt like heaven.

My trembling hand clanged the glass on the table. That clink woke me out of my daydream. My waiter now stood beside the table and I sensed he had a questioning look on his face, but I remembered quite clearly that I had paid the bill.

I made a special effort to look alert and sober as I said, "No, I'm fine, nothing else."

I tried to take care that no one saw me as I carefully stood and touched several empty tables for support while making my way to the door. Fortunately, I didn't see anyone looking in my direction.

Once outside, I was grateful for the cold spring air. However, as I tried to move my body, my knees were trembling. I managed to get off the sidewalk, into the alley beside the building, before I fell. I was aware I had hit cold cement. However, I didn't feel anything, since I had blacked out.

"Mrs. Brady, Mrs. Brady, it's you!"

I regained consciousness and realized that Mike the doorman was squatting near me, looking worried. He must have just been on his way home after his shift.

He lifted me and carried me to the edge of the sidewalk, where he carefully placed me in his parked car.

"This is a cold night for you to be out," Mike said. I felt grateful to him for pretending that I had simply been walking along as I'd intended to do, and not curled up in an alley.

My teeth were chattering, but I did manage to utter a shaky, "Thank you, Mike."

In a moment, Mike pulled up to our apartment building, where Sol, the late shift doorman, helped him get me to the elevator. The three of us went up to the 10th floor.

I put my arms around their shoulders as they helped me move my numb, wobbly legs down the hall and into my apartment.

Before our eyes was a sleeping Claudette, a bottle of Scotch and an ice-filled glass on the table next to her. Rushing into my bedroom, I was relieved to see Jeriann safely sleeping in our bed. In the living room, Mike and Sol roused Claudette, who was clearly drunk. I wanted to yell at her, but I could hardly make sound come from my mouth. I had the passing thought that perhaps it was divine justice I could not do any shouting, since my behavior on this night matched hers.

Sol said to Claudette, "How could you sit here drunk, and fall asleep on the job, when you're supposed to be taking care of Mrs. Brady's little girl?"

Claudette acted offended and claimed that she wasn't drunk in the least. When Mike touched her elbow to help her get out of the chair, she pushed his hand away.

"I don't know what you are all making such a fuss about!" she said, trying to muster her dignity. "I have done my duty here, and Miss Brady is safe and sound in her bed. You have no right to accuse me of anything! I will call the police!"

"We should call the police ourselves," Mike said, with a disgusted look on his face.

Sol helped me sit down on the couch. "Mrs. Brady, since Mike is off duty, he will make sure your sitter gets home, and I'll stay here and get you settled."

Claudette started to cry as she put on her coat and followed Mike out the door.

"Wait a minute!" I said. I reached into my purse and paid Claudette what I owed her. I felt that, even though she had made an awful mistake, and I would never hire her again, I had made similar mistakes of my own, including that very night.

By now I had started to come to my senses. I told Sol, "I am ever so grateful that you and Mike saved me tonight."

Sol looked at me with concern and sympathy. "Oh, Mrs. Brady, think nothing of it, but if you need anything just ring me up. I'll be right at my station by the front door."

Sol's kindness, and my own relief, brought tears to my eyes. After Sol left, I soaked in a hot bath, and then crawled into Jerry's and my safe and secure bed, beside Jeriann. Hearing her breathing, and knowing she was alright, I felt better than I had felt in a long time. I made a decision, right then and there, that I should have made over a year earlier. I fell asleep, happy in the knowledge that I now knew what I had to do.

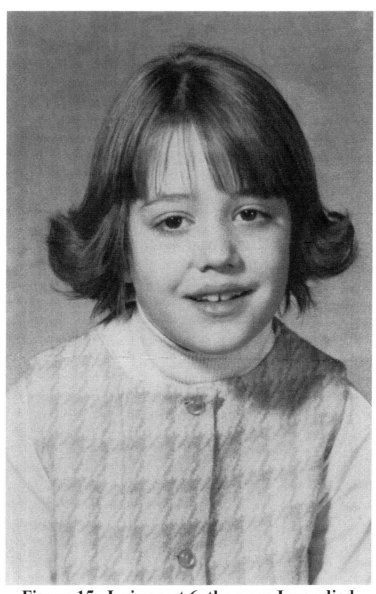

Figure 15: Jeriann at 6, the year Jerry died

23: Goodbye to New York

In the morning, the sun streamed through the half-open Venetian blinds on the double windows in our bedroom. At the Chinese restaurant, the night before, my memories had been of Jerry as a vital, strong man. In the light of day, my memories were of Jerry as I caressed his frail sixty pound body. How different he had become, but my love had still been passionate. The Venetian blinds were in the same position as they had been on the morning when Jerry had died. With a blessed kind of joy, I remembered what he had said to Jeriann a few days earlier.

"My darling little girl, Jeriann, I hope you grow up to be a sweet, warm and loving woman like your mother."

I certainly had not acted like a sweet woman, as I drank those martinis and then fell to the cement in an alley! What would Jerry have thought of his Deany, if he could have seen me like that? What would he have said about Masako, or about the way I had let all our friendships go?

I realized that the side of my head hurt, where I must have hit the pavement, and one of my shoulders ached too. Pushing back the coverlet, I saw a bruise on my hip, reminding me of the moment when Jerry's white Cadillac had bumped into me as I jaywalked across Collins Avenue in Miami Beach.

313

Something happened right then that I will never forget. I suddenly became gloriously flooded with the sound of Jerry's strong, warm voice, speaking to me as clearly as if he were in the room.

"My dear Deany," he said, "instead of remaining consumed with images of me in the past, look instead at Jeriann's sweet face beside you and cast your gaze toward happy future years to be shared with her."

I felt as if I had been struck with lightning, Jerry's presence was so near and so vivid. I jumped from our bed, filled with an electric alertness and longing. Could Jerry really have spoken to me? Could he really be here in spirit?

Jeriann woke up and lay in bed smiling, yawning and stretching. I bent down and grabbed her with a big hug, as I felt my heart thumping wildly against her thin, warm body. I absolutely knew, as if by magic, that through this remarkable spiritual experience of Jerry's presence, I had become released from the agonizing pain and grief that had consumed me for so many months.

"My darling Jeriann, the most amazing thing has happened."

Jeriann looked into my eyes. "What happened, Mommy?"

I sat next to her on the bed and stroked her hair.

"A message came to me as I woke up just now, and it seemed as if your Daddy was telling me something."

Jeriann's face brightened. "What did Daddy say?"

"Well, I felt like he said you and I should go back to Georgia and live with Best Mama and Pop."

She flung her arms around my neck, and held tight, saying, "Oh, Mommy, Mommy, Mommy, are you sure?"

Then I saw the familiar hesitant look come into her face. It was as if she was trying to understand the way I really felt in that moment. Even though she was so young, she always wanted to make sure to please me.

She asked again, just above a whisper, "Are you sure, Mommy?" Her pretty face was filled with a mixture of shy happiness and worry.

And I answered, "Yes, I'm sure! I already have a plan in place. Come, let's have breakfast while I tell you about my plan."

I took her comforting, soft little hand and we entered the kitchen. I had toast, an egg and coffee -- a much healthier breakfast than I had become used to that year -- while Jeriann hungrily consumed her bowl of cornflakes, milk and sliced banana. She kept casting her eyes up to mine, expectantly. It came to me that this was the first time we had sat at the kitchen table to eat a meal together since her father's passing.

With breakfast finished, she went to the sink, placed her bowl and spoon in the dishwasher, and came back to lean her slender body against me. As I embraced her, and smelled the fragrance of her hair as it brushed my nose, I began to feel great joy and strength infusing my entire being. I wondered why I had felt so urgently the need to be always rushing around, striving for material success. It was as though I was awakening from a dream that had imprisoned me.

315

"I'm so glad you have your Dad's brown hair and you're not a cotton-top child like me, when I was your age."

She looked up into my face and those smiling brown eyes seemed to indicate how proud she was that she looked like her Daddy.

"Now dear, I want you to help me get rid of some unneeded baggage. Please go to your play room and bring your little red wagon to the liquor cabinet. We are going to load all those bottles of alcohol into your wagon and take them to the garbage chute, and we are going to toss them down it."

She rushed off and returned, pulling her wagon. In silence, I handed her the bottles and she placed them in the wagon.

I said, "These bottles are all almost empty," to which she replied, "Yes, I've been seeing the bottles there for a long time."

I hoped she would never know how many times I had replaced the empty bottles with full ones.

I motioned to Jeriann to follow me, and we marched to the back hall, where the residents on our floor put their garbage into the chute. I will always remember my daughter looking carefully up at me each time she placed a bottle in the chute, as I held the little door open. She clearly understood the huge importance of this ceremony, but she couldn't seem to figure out just what it meant. The clanging of each bottle as it bounced back and forth against the chute's interior, diving ten floors to the bottom of the receptacle, definitely humbled me. I prayed for a higher score in parenting during the coming years than I had earned since Jerry's death.

That evening, we telephoned Mommy and Daddy to share the good news that in two weeks we would be coming home to live. Their voices were chiming with such joy, I could hardly understand the words they spoke, so I handed the phone to Jeriann. From the sound of her responses, the three of them were on the same wave length and understood each other perfectly.

The following two weeks flew by in a flurry of preparation. Each day, as soon as we finished breakfast, Jeriann's joyful, jumping skips couldn't help but lift my spirits as we walked hand in hand to her school, before I went home to pack more boxes.

Once Jeriann realized that she had only a few days left of school, she asked, "Mommy, may I sit with you in the office while you tell Mrs. Scott I'm going home to Georgia?" Mrs. Scott was the head of Jeriann's small private school. I wondered if Jeriann worried that I might change my mind.

"Yes," I said, "you may come with me tomorrow morning to talk to Mrs. Scott first thing."

When I told Masako I was closing the business, she surprised me by saying she had already begun a plan for her and her daughters to return to Japan. The remaining days of our relationship were cordial. I saw very little of her, since I had power of attorney to make all decisions regarding the closing of the business. I was very grateful to the lawyers of Jerry's estate, and to the Executors, Ed and

Nat, who handled everything, so that I didn't have to deal with any paperwork.

I decided to place most of our household belongings into storage, while Jeriann and I made this transition. My parents' house wouldn't be large enough to fit all our furniture, clothes and art, and I knew I would be able to ship some of these items to us in the future, if I wished. In any case, I felt so eager to go home; I couldn't imagine sifting through all the contents of our life with Jerry, and bringing his loss to the fore again. So I opened the Yellow Pages of the New York City telephone directory and did an "eeny, meeny, miny, moe" with my finger until it paused on "Moe." I immediately called that company, and the date was set for the removal of all my belongings into storage.

One beautiful morning in June, Jeriann and I were seated in a taxicab, heading for Idlewild Airport. Crossing the Triborough Bridge, I looked back at the skyline of New York City and my eyes filled with tears.

Jeriann saw my sadness and began to sob and hug me.

"I thought you were happy going to live with Best Mama and Pop. Why are you crying? I'm not happy when you're not happy."

I dried my tears and smiled, thinking how much that remark reminded me of her Daddy. That was just one of many happy reminders of Jerry, with which Jeriann would be delighting me during the blessed years following, and even until this day.

"I'm happy, Jeriann," I said. "I really am. This is the best thing to do, going home again to Georgia. It's just that I've loved living in New York with your Daddy and you. We had a wonderful life together, while we could."

Jeriann looked at me seriously. "Daddy got sick, though."

I nodded. "Yes, Daddy got sick, and he couldn't keep on living with us."

She put her little hand on mine, and gave me a few pats.

"We'll have fun with Best Mama and Pop, Mommy."

I laughed and hugged her close. "Yes, we will! I guess this city will always be in me, in any case. They can take me out of New York, but they can never take New York out of me."

Jeriann nodded. "But I like Georgia best," she said.

She and I started a game of counting all the good things we liked at her Best Mama's and Pop's house, and before we knew it, we were at the airport.

A few hours later, as our plane approached Atlanta, Jeriann and I looked out the window together at the vast rolling spread of green forested mountains. I could feel those beloved mountains welcoming me home, just as they had the first time I had descended from the air. That sad return had been for the burial of my precious Grandma, she who had so dearly loved me and cuddled me in her lap with her strong arms around me on many nights, while we listened to the winds whistling through the tall pines growing on the mountain tops.

319

I remembered how Grandma had often pointed to Yonder Mountain, the one rising so high up, above all the surrounding hills and ridges.

"Grandma," I would say sometimes, "I want to go even higher than Yonder Mountain."

"Bless me, Odean," she would say, giving me a squeeze and a kiss, "you are a young dreamer. Can't you be content with life right here in our neighborhood, and on our farm? Look at all you have here -- your Mommy and Daddy, your Grandma, your sister and brother, and all the animals and fields, and the stream you love to wade in."

Gazing at the rolling green out the airplane window, over Jeriann's small head, I thought about how, in my life with Jerry, I had indeed had the chance to float and soar above all that I had ever known. I remembered my wedding night, as I looked out our penthouse window, and realized that the Delmonico was so much higher than my old, familiar Yonder Mountain. Yet here I was, coming back to my original home.

Descending into the Atlanta Airport, I whispered to my Grandma, "I wish you could have seen your beloved mountains as I'm seeing them, descending from the air. Now, these many years later, I wish you could see me as I'm bringing home your great-granddaughter Jeriann, so my Mommy can love and cuddle her as you did me, while she grows up in the old mountain home place."

Once inside the Atlanta Airport, I stood at the baggage counter, relishing the joy of seeing my parents and Jeriann delighting the onlookers with their love-fest.

As Daddy drove down Northside Drive, heading toward Ellijay, I breathed a prayerful sigh of relief and my heart filled with happy expectations. Sitting cozily among our bags in the back seat of the Ford Fairlane, I began to feel the relief of knowing that my parenting responsibilities would be shared with my Daddy and Mommy. Jeriann was up front in Mommy's lap, being embraced and comforted by my mother's loving arms.

I caught a glimmer of a realization that maybe I could find something inspiring in this return to my roots in Gilmer County, GA. Instead of running away from myself, as I had been doing, maybe I could simply enjoy my daughter and face my life with honesty and compassion. I promised myself that I would try as hard as I could to make good use of whatever wisdom I could find. I had in earlier days danced among the sparkles of Jerry and his brilliant friends. This time I would make every effort to find the real me by looking inward to the core of my being. I would look again within that little barefoot Appalachian child's heart.

I think it was in the car that day, heading home to Ellijay, that I first had an inkling I really might one day start to become a writer. I held close my memory of Mr. Hagan and all his hopes for me. Anything was possible.

24: Home Again

Jeriann and I basked in the comfort and love of my parents' household. That first year, I felt blessed to see my daughter progress beyond my prayerful expectations. Thank heavens she felt immensely cared for by those two special people in her life. She made steady progress in second grade, attending Oakland School, where my ancestors and siblings and I had received our early schooling. It was through the patient work of Bonnie Norris, her second grade teacher that Jeriann caught up and excelled.

Years later, Jeriann often visited Miss Bonnie in her nursing on her trips back to Georgia. She told Miss Bonnie that when she was catching up on her reading and writing that school year, she had decided that she'd become a second grade teacher someday, because she wanted to help struggling students as Miss Bonnie had helped her – and she did.

As an added benefit of our move, Jeriann also had many more friends in Ellijay than she had had in New York. These included my brother Gene's children, Beth and William, as well as my sister Colleen's grandson, Chris. Beth and William lived next door, and were like a sister and brother to her. Beth and Jeriann would roam for hours, totally free, swimming in the creek and raising baby calves on a bottle. Jeriann went from being a shy, troubled, lonely little girl who couldn't read, to a strong, healthy, confident girl, who loved school and made good friends.

During this time of healing and renewal, my grief for Jerry started to transform into gratitude for his presence in Jeriann's, my parents', and my life. I was sure that Jerry would have been proud of me, as I helped my parents in the fields and the gardens, milked the cows, and threw bales of hay off the tractor for the cows to eat. I felt happy wearing plaid shirts and work clothes, instead of the silk and linen outfits I had worn in Miami Beach and New York. I remembered how Jerry would say he wished he could live as healthily as I had in my childhood, with all that fresh air and sunshine, and now I was living that life again with our little girl.

I spent a lot of time blissfully on my own, looking for calves that had been born in the pasture, herding the cows in for their milking, or simply walking in the woods and sitting by my beloved stream. I felt amazed at the way I could start listening to the world around me, and to my own inner spirit. I still missed Jerry, but I was increasingly relieved to have let that other life of parties and champagne go. Here I could start to be truly myself. It has been a journey that continues to this day.

One of my happiest memories of that time in Georgia is of listening to Jeriann talking with her Best Mama (Jerry's thought of that name). My Mommy was one of the best listeners in the world, in addition to being one of the best storytellers, and she helped my daughter sift through and understand her young years.

324

One day some years later, as I was paying some bills inside my bedroom, I heard Jeriann and my mother talking comfortably on the porch outside my window, as they strung beans for the afternoon canning. Though occasionally the screeching of Daddy's file drowned their soft voices, as he sharpened his power saw at the other end of the porch, I could hear some of their friendly conversation.

Mommy's soft voice came through my bedroom window.

"Jeriann, do you remember much about living in New York?"

"No, Best Mama, not much about New York. I do remember a lot about being with Daddy and him always playing with me. He read stories to me, and we did puzzles and played games. I loved him taking me in my red wagon to the toy store down the street."

"That sounds like fun," Mommy said.

"Oh, it was."

"What else do you remember?"

"I remember being on Daddy's shoulders as we stood on the sidewalk and watched the Macy's Christmas Parade each year. That was before we moved to our apartment in Miami Beach."

"And do you have memories of your winters in Miami Beach?"

"Oh, yes, I do remember more about Daddy there. I think it's because we were always playing together in the pool or Daddy holding me tight when we would rush into the big ocean waves."

I felt so glad that Jeriann remembered her Daddy in this way, and I vowed to continue sharing these stories with her, so she could always know how greatly Jerry had loved her.

25: Memories Restored

One spring day, a year or so after we had moved home, I took my usual walk up and over the hill to our mailbox on the main road. Among the bills and flyers, I discovered one of my own envelopes to the storage company in New Jersey. The address had a line through it, with the words "Addressee Unknown."

Opening the envelope in disbelief, I took out my most recent monthly check for storage. I had no idea how to get in touch with the company. New York felt so big and far away. The check fell out of my limp hand and into the mud, as I stood dumbfounded, leaning on the mailbox post for support.

A dark thunderstorm started moving fast toward me. Slipping and sliding up the red muddy road, I reached the top of the hill. With our house in sight through the newly budding leaves, I paused in the rain to look down at the pasture near our home. Something in the fresh air and the fragrance of the wet earth comforted me. I thought to myself, my life here was complete, and I could do without most of the items from our apartment in New York. However, I had stored valuable diaries, letters and photographs, which I keenly wished could be restored to me.

I postponed mention of my storage to anyone, including Jeriann. I decided I would tell her one day, but in the meantime I was happy to move on, into the life she and I were creating now.

Years passed. One day I received a call from Jeriann, who was by now married and living in California.

"You could never guess what I'm holding in my hand!" Jeriann said after I answered the phone, "It's a box from your storage in New York!"

I felt stunned.

"How could you have that? Everything I had was lost years ago," I blurted out.

"I know, but a man phoned Uncle Gene and said he had bought a trunk at a second hand shop in New York about twenty years ago. When he looked at the contents of the trunk - the photographs, the letters, a diary - he knew in his heart that the person those items belonged to never meant for them to get lost. And he was determined to someday return them to the owner or at least to the little girl in the photos.

"Uncle Gene said the man had been amazed when he read a friendly letter to Daddy from J. Edgar Hoover, complimenting him on the birth of his daughter! Uncle Gene couldn't help laughing, when he told me what the man said: 'I didn't know J. Edgar Hoover *had* a friend!'"

Hearing that made me chuckle, as I remembered Jerry's colorful and wide-ranging group of friends.

"Tell me more!"

I could hear Jeri taking a deep breath.

"This man searched for twenty years for the owner of this trunk! He found letters suggesting that a person who had owned the trunk had a partner named Masako Hoshino. There was a telephone number beside her name, so he called her."

I squeezed the phone as I held it to my ear, which was now burning like fire. "Go on," I whispered.

"Well, after introducing himself to this woman and giving the reason for his call, he asked her, 'Did you have a partner in a boutique, named Dean Brady?' He said she was silent for a long moment, and then she told him, 'Yes, but sadly, she is dead.'"

A flicker of my old distress and anger rose up in me.

"Being truthful was not a strong point with her!"

"The man said that ended his search in New York and he boxed up the papers and photos. At some point, he moved back to St. Louis for several years, but he just could not trash that box. Every time he moved and came across the box he made an attempt to find the family of the owner but was never successful. He moved again, this time to Richmond, Virginia, and again the box came with him. Finally he moved to Georgia and remembered there were some letters from a brother in Georgia."

"Georgia?'

I could sense Jeriann smiling. "Yes, Georgia."

"But why didn't Gene tell me?"

"Just listen! In going through the box again, this man found a letter to you with the name and return address of your brother, Gene Warren, in Ellijay. He looked in the Ellijay telephone book and called him. Uncle Gene told the man that he was welcome to send the box to him and he would take care of it."

"But why didn't Gene tell me himself?"

Jeriann hesitated a moment, and then she said, "Uncle Gene thought the box might make you sad, so instead of telling you about it, he called me and then mailed it to California, so I would have a chance to look inside it first, and make sure you would like to have it again."

I realized that my family still felt protective of me, and I felt grateful and frustrated at the same time.

"Anyway, the important thing is, the box came today! And Mom, it has good stuff in it, mostly pictures of me and Daddy - one at a swimming pool. It also has a diary where you mention celebrity friends of Daddy and you."

I became ecstatic, but could not speak.

Jeriann almost shouted into the phone, "I can't wait for you to see this and tell me all the stories that go with the pictures!"

On the day when Jeriann and I finally had the chance to pore over all the contents of this box together, I felt stunned with happiness and sadness, mixed together. In the photographs, Jerry looked his handsome self, as he laughed with friends or held Jeriann as a baby and toddler. My diaries, too, brought back shining details

330

of our life together, both with our friends and as a family. As Jeriann asked me questions about the photos and diaries, it struck me powerfully that this was indeed my chance to start writing the stories down, just as she so wished I would do. Over the course of the following years, those stories would grow into my first memoir, *An Appalachian Childhood*, and then into this one, *Higher than Yonder Mountain*.

During the nearly fifty years since my life in New York ended, my heart has frequently overflowed with joy and gratitude, remembering all those marvelous years that I was privileged to enjoy. My heady love affair and marriage to my Prince culminated in Jerry giving me the greatest gift, our precious daughter Jeriann. Often now as I help Jeriann in her classroom, or go with her to one of my grandson's baseball games, I can just imagine Jerry's pride in our daughter's compassion and insight. I can almost hear Jerry saying, "Deany, what a wonderful daughter you have raised, with the help of her Best Mama and Pop."

One August, about ten years ago, for my anniversary present, Jeriann and her husband David bought tickets for all of us to fly to New York City and revisit my old "hangout" places. At first I was reluctant to accept this gift, since there was no one now living who had graced my life in those early days. Luckily, however, I decided to go with Jeriann and David on this adventure. Our vacation was highlighted by the pleasure of pushing my grandson,

Brady's stroller through all the areas where Jerry and I had spent so many happy days with Jeriann.

On that trip, I enjoyed seeing many of the majestic buildings I had known so well: the Delmonico, the Plaza, the Ritz, and of course Henri Soule's restaurant Le Pavillon, at 111 E. 57th St. The Pavillon's space is now a Borders bookstore; however, standing outside, pressing my nose against the glass window, I sensed time melting away. I did not see the books lined up in neat rows on the shelves, because I had a replay in my mind of those glorious evenings when Jerry and I celebrated with our friends the Sullivans, and many more.

I felt the warmth of Jeriann's hand holding mine and I saw the face of my dear son-in-law smiling at me as I bent to kiss the top of Brady's head. Then I motioned us onward, and together we walked over to Central Park, to show Brady the zoo. I decided to take them to the Plaza for lunch, and pop in to FAO Schwartz for a toy or book for Brady. And I looked forward to returning to our home in California, within sight of the beautiful green Foothills near Sunnyvale, and to our home in Georgia too, where Brady could wade in Turkey Creek as it flowed past our old Appalachian home.

Afterword

I lived on our family farm, after Jerry died, for much of the following 25 years. My precious Mommy passed away in 1982 as Jeriann was beginning college. Daddy and I spent quality time together on the farm during the years after Mommy's death, while I dove with head and heart into studying and growing spiritually. Just as I had hoped, when Jeriann and I first moved back to Georgia, I began to uncover layers of spiritual growth inside me. For Daddy it became a time of contentment and peace, except on the days when he was determined to climb up on the seat of that formerly red tractor - now rusty and scraped up because of years of constant use. Daddy and I rejoiced to see Jeriann and David on their regular visits to the farm.

In 1995, two years after the discovery of the box of pictures and diaries, my sweet Daddy died. Jeriann and David invited me to move to Sunnyvale to live with them, and I gladly said yes. It was time to start a new chapter of my life, with the people dearest to my heart.

The farmhouse and land in Georgia have existed in a constant state of renewal. After I moved to California we rented the farmhouse. One family in particular, Terry and Rodney, lived in and cared for the house for years. They kept a room ready for our visit each summer. Our friends Tom and Francie continue to keep a watchful eye on the property and bush hog it when we forget. So many people have expressed interest in seeing the farmhouse that we are working on restoring, rebuilding, and sharing it as a vacation rental with those who know its story.

Jeriann and David now have a son, Brady (named after my Prince). Most summers I have had the great pleasure of seeing my grandson dip his toes in the rushing water, just as his Mom did when she was a little girl, and Colleen, Gene and I did before her. As I hold hands with my daughter and grandson, we wade around the same rocks where I waded each summer of my childhood. The music of the small waterfalls is the same now as when my Great-great-grandfather was alive. This sound speaks to my heart of the eternity of being.

Acknowledgments

My daughter Jeriann Hirsch and her husband David, who is like a son to me, have encouraged me constantly to write with honesty and courage. Jeriann has combed through my stories with her clear eye, cheering me on with that quality so honored by Mr. Hagan -- enthusiasm. I could not have written my first two memoirs without these two precious family members. I look forward to writing a third memoir soon, *An Examined Life*, about our life together in California with my grandson Brady, and my continuing search for spiritual growth.

I very much appreciate Principals Linda Creighton and Nancy Hendry, of Laurel Elementary School, who have kindly allowed me to volunteer several days each week for the past twenty years in Jeriann's second grade classroom. This constant interaction with the children and teachers keeps me feeling useful and inspired. Cherishing happy hours at school during the day enables me to spend fruitful evening hours slipping back in time and sorting out details of my past life and placing them on the page. I am also grateful to the hundreds of parents in the Menlo Park School System who have purchased my memoir and recommended it to others.

Many of these parents have generously hosted me as a book club guest in their homes for *An Appalachian Childhood*.

I am thankful to all the bookstores and festivals in which I have presented my memoirs. Kepler's Books in Menlo Park, California has been especially generous in their support. Following the special day of book signing in their fabulous castle of books, to launch *An Appalachian Childhood*, Kepler's has graciously invited me back for the launch of *Higher than Yonder Mountain*.

My love and gratitude abounds to the citizens of my birthplace, Ellijay, Georgia, who honored me as Grand Marshall of the Apple Festival parade. Special thanks go to the daughter of one of my childhood friends, Lena Kennemur Reece. Lynelle Reece Stewart, Lena's daughter, and Lynelle's husband Stan, have extended to me an open invitation to spend time in their lovely historic home when I'm back in Ellijay for book signings. Also, my many thanks to the Ellijay Library and to merchants and Apple Houses in and near Ellijay who carry my book.

My heart floods with gratitude to my dear editor and writing coach, Harriet Scott Chessman, who has so patiently guided me over the years, as she worked with me to create my books. Without Harriet my books would have remained an impossible dream. With her assistance, this learning adventure has been a most fulfilling and rewarding experience. With all my heart, thank you, Harriet.

336

Dawn Edgren offered major help in the copy editing of this memoir. I am so appreciative of Dawn's careful, insightful and expert work. Lynn Murphy has been a constant support during the writing of both of my books. Thank you for all our editing dinners.

The art for the covers of both my books was exquisitely done by London artist, Julie Tennent Dene, who is a descendant of J. M. W. Turner. Julie and Jeriann became fast sister-friends during their boarding school years together near London. Many thanks, precious Julie, from me, your adopted American auntie.

I also wish to acknowledge the inspiration that has come to me all my life from the landscape of my childhood. This summer, as always, I hope to be writing my thoughts and memories on a pad of paper as I sit by Turkey Creek and dabble my feet in the water, listening to the birds in the trees and to Jeriann and Brady splashing nearby. Brady too, loves those majestic mountains that have been home to him, as well as to Jeriann and me, my Dad and Mom, my Grandma, and her father and mother, going back to the 1850s.

Brady, who is helping plan the building of a new home on the site of the old one, has expressed this desire to his parents: "I hope the house has two stories, so that I can be nearer the top of Yonder Mountain."

About the Author

Figure 16: Deany honored as the Grand Marshall in the 2014 Ellijay Apple Festival Parade[1]

In 1996 Deany moved to Silicon Valley to be with her daughter, son-in-law, and her grandson Brady. She attended college for a while, began a 20+ year career at Whole Foods Market, and volunteered as an aide in her daughter's second grade classroom. Since publishing her first book, *An Appalachian Childhood*, Deany has enjoyed being invited as a book club guest, holding book signings, and answering emails (deanybrady@yahoo.com) about her book.

---

[1] Courtesy of Times-Courier

Figure 17: A Return Visit to Central Park with Jeriann and Brady

Figure 18: At one of the book signings

Figure 19: A Guest at a local book club meeting

Made in the USA
San Bernardino, CA
16 February 2017